Practices That Work

Bringing Learners to Professional Proficiency in World Languages

Thomas Jesús Garza, Ed. D.
Editor

For information, contact
MSI Press LLC
1760-F Airline Hwy, #203
Hollister, CA 95023

Front cover design: Carl D. Leaver
Back cover design: Opeyemi Ikuborije
Layout & typesetting: Opeyemi Ikuborije

Library of Congress Control Number: 2021946954
ISBN 978-1-950328-67-3

Dedication

This 2021 revised edition, *Practices That Work: Bringing Learners to Professional Proficiency in World Languages*, is dedicated to the memory of two colleagues whose contributions to language education and advanced proficiency is dwarfed only by their generosity of spirit.

Boris V. Shekhtman (1939-2017)
Madeline E. Ehrman (1942-2015)

Thomas Jesús Garza, Ed. D.

CONTENTS

Section I: Focus on the Learner

Section II: Focus on Instruction

Section III: Focus on the Instructor

Section IV: Focus on Skills

Section V: Focus on Assessment

Acknowledgments

In 2002,[1] the Coalition of Distinguished Language Centers was established to promote the teaching of world languages to the highest levels of proficiency: ACTFL Advanced High to Distinguished / ILR levels 2+ to 5. The current volume is indebted to the groundbreaking work of Betty Lou Leaver and Boris Shekhtman and their colleagues at the CDLC who moved this lofty goal from aspirational to attainable and paved the way for cooperation between government and university programs in this effort. We gratefully acknowledge their many contributions.

---

[1] The CDLC closed in 2010, but most of those associated with it have continued to promote near-native proficiency in a variety of other venues.

Thomas Jesús Garza, Ed. D.

Introduction

This volume represents a revised and expanded version of the 2008 first edition titled What Works: Helping Students Reach Native-Like Second-Language Competence and includes, in addition to all of the excellent original contributions[2], eleven new pieces from language practitioners with experience in Language Flagship Programs and/or university programs with established records of success in bringing learners to Professional-level proficiency in languages. Like its predecessor, this new edition seeks to offer the reader a broad selection of tested, successful models of practice from classrooms in both government and post-secondary institutions that have attested results of professional proficiency among its learners. Its intended audience is the language practitioner who understands that the goal of attaining high-level proficiency is possible and is looking for new or additional ways and means to enhance their courses with field-tested "formulas" for learner success.

This new edition adds to the combined practices of our colleagues with experiences garnered over the last decade. What is common in their experience, -however, is the commitment to bring their learners to high-level professional proficiency. Many of the newer contributions to this volume are from instructors in university language Flagship programs: federally funded programs that support the attainment of high-level proficiency for undergraduate and graduate students for all academic disciplines.

---

[2] Contributors to the original volume whose contributions have been included in this volume are identified in accordance with the positions they held at the time that they wrote their original contribution.

The inauguration of the Language Flagship program, a federally-funded component of the National Security Education Program (NSEP) at the U.S. Department of Defense, in 2002 marked the ambitious reset of the goal of a four-year college or university language program from "functional" to "professional" proficiency, i.e., from the ACTFL Intermediate to the Advanced High level and beyond. Through proficiency-oriented, standards-based training, combined with an incountry capstone and internship program, Flagship programs began producing graduates with the desired results. The sea change that the Flagship experience brought to the postsecondary language teaching community is reflected not only in the attainment of high levels of proficiency among learners but also in the professional experience of the instructors in these programs, showing promising progress from the situation described in the comment in the 2008 edition of this volume, "Teachers with high-level proficiency teaching experience are, indeed, a nearly microscopic subset of the body of foreign language teachers in the USA and abroad." The field of language teaching has benefitted from the increasing focus on attaining professional proficiency and, in turn, our students have profited from the expanded offerings of high-level courses.

The volume is divided into five sections which group the practices by their focus: Learner, Instruction, Instructor, Skills, and Assessment. Section I: Focus on the Learner offers models of learner-centered practices that can promote autonomous learning and proficiency gains. Section II: Focus on Instruction and Section III: Focus on the Instructor provide, respectively, models of classroom practices that have produced Superior-level speakers of the language and share recommendations for instructors in these courses to help them create the kinds of materials and learning environments that will foster ever higher proficiency gains. Section IV: Focus on Skills gives concrete examples of teaching strategies and techniques that have succeeded in producing high-level proficiency outcomes in a variety of settings and with various languages. Finally, Focus on Assessment demonstrates formats and techniques to measure and evaluate learner progress during our courses of study. Each "formula" ends with a list of readings that includes any works cited as well as other works that can reflect greater insight or more information on the topic of the "formula."

Together, these "formulas"—some short, some longer, depending on topic and experience with the topic—comprise a kind of go-to handbook for instructors looking for new ideas, techniques, or inspiration to help their learners attain professional proficiency in a world language and culture. Most of the "formulas" are language-generic, but they come from experience with Arabic, Chinese, English (ESL/EFL), French, German, Portuguese, Russian, and Spanish, representing one or more languages from each of the U.S. government's four language categories (based on observed and tracked difficulty of acquisition).

The 2008 first edition of this book stated its two-fold purpose as: 1) to show that bringing learners to professional proficiency in world languages in U.S. program could be done; and 2) to show how these results could be attained. This 2021 revised version reiterates these original purposes and adds one more: 3) to demonstrate why world language education must be part of every educational curriculum and part of every U.S. citizen's consciousness. The attainment of professional proficiency in world languages is a game changer for international relations and diplomacy, global business, medicine, education, and a host of other fields for which communication and mutual understanding is paramount. Let us seize this opportunity to change the timbre and tone of the U.S. presence abroad through cadres of well-educated and fully proficient global professionals through high-level language and culture education.

Comparison of ILR to ACTFL Scale

ACTFL Scale

- Distinguished

- Superior

- Advanced High
- Advanced Mid
- Advanced Low

- Intermediate High
- Intermediate Mid
- Intermediate Low

- Novice High
- Novice Mid
- Novice Low

ILR Scale

- 5 Functionally Native Proficiency
- 4+ Advanced Professional Proficiency Plus
- 4 Advanced Professional Proficiency
- 3+ General Professional Proficiency Plus
- 3 General Professional Proficiency

- 2+ Limited Working Proficiency Plus
- 2 Limited Working Proficiency

- 1+ Elementary Proficiency Plus
- 1 Elementary Proficiency

- 0+ Memorized Proficiency

- 0 No Proficiency

Section I

Focus on the Learner

Thomas Jesús Garza, Ed. D.

1

Individualize the Learning Plan

Betty Lou Leaver
(Defense Language Institute Foreign Language Center)

Recent qualitative and quantitative research with high-level proficient language users that addresses the question, "How Did I Do It?" consistently points to one irrefutable and very important fact: there are nearly as many paths to professional proficiency as there are near-native language users. Further, high-level polyglots (those individuals who have reached professional, native-like proficiency in more than one language) report different—sometimes highly divergent—paths for reaching professional proficiency in each of their languages. This variation in paths to success leads to two conclusions generally shared by high-level teachers. The first has to do with methodology, the second with language planning as part of the teaching process.

The evidence is quite clear that no specific teaching method will bring a learner from Novice to Distinguished level. While many of the teachers whose work is summarized in this volume have been leaders in the development of the theories and practices behind today's cutting-edge methods, such as content-based instruction, task-based instruction, and the looser concept of proficiency-based methods, and use liberal doses of them in their classrooms, none of these have been shown to bring learners to native-like proficiency although content-based instruction, when combined with real-life classroom tasks, can help learners more quickly approach the Superior level—but only if combined with diagnostic assessment and a healthy dose of diagnostic teaching (learner-based instruction).

Further, the evidence is also clear that what works in English as a Second Language may be less effective in Arabic, Chinese, French, German, or Russian as a Second Language. In other words, while teachers of various languages can add to the dialogue of how best to teach a language, the successful practices of one set of language teachers cannot necessarily adequately inform the practices of teachers of another language. Learning Russian or Arabic *is* different from learning English or French, and vice versa.

Any teacher who has taught high-level language successfully and has acquired high-level proficiency in multiple languages knows this phenomenon; so do polyglots, who frequently state that they used different methods for learning different languages because the nature of the languages themselves required such an approach. Some of this variation is because semantics are language-specific, as are cultural phenomena and even "mentality" (ways of thinking). Some of it is because the nature of the linguistic systems used to make meaning differs in very significant ways that have a clear impact on acquisition: where there are parallels with one's own language, the system is usually more quickly acquired; where there are imperfect parallels, native-language schemata must be adapted; and where there is no overlap at all, new schemata must be developed. For this reason, it is typically more difficult for a speaker of English to acquire a language like Arabic or Chinese, and in turn, the teaching methods and tools for assisting learners in acquiring English are less likely to be as effective for assisting learners in acquiring languages that are not closely related in semantics, syntax, morphology, mechanisms for showing structural and functional relationships among lexemes, and "where" to look for meaning. Thus, a single, universal method for language acquisition is not likely to be effective, especially if it denies the importance of other methods in bringing Superior-level learners to Distinguished-level proficiency.

Learners took differing approaches to successful acquisition of high-level language also based on their learning styles. Learners with thin boundaries (those who tend to merge thought and emotions and easily accept external influences) were often quicker to look for a friend from the other culture to lead them to sociolinguistic and sociocultural competence than were learners with thick boundaries who preferred to glean this information from movies, books, and observation from a distance. Ectenic learners (those who learn atomistically, in bottom-up ways) were more likely to reach the Superior level with "clean" language, i.e., language free of mis-speaking and mis-typing, than synoptic learners although the latter generally have reached the Superior level with a better "feel" for the language. All learners have a different task to accomplish in perfecting their language to the point of being considered near-native in proficiency.

Some learners have been born with a talent for language. In some cases, it is an intuitive understanding of linguistic structure; in other cases, it is a "good ear." Other learners have more moderate language aptitude. Yet, all have reached professional levels of proficiency in their own language, and even learners with moderate (or lower) scores on language aptitude tests are represented among those in the elite group that has achieved Superior and Distinguished levels of language proficiency.

Languages were learned in different ways also because serendipity led individuals to have differing opportunities while in language study. Some individuals had home or community environments where another language was spoken. Others had reached the Advanced level before an opportunity to travel abroad appeared. Some were surrounded by émigré communities; others were isolated and depended on pen-pals and, today's learners, the Internet.

Essentially, for each learner who desires to reach native-like professional proficiency, there needs to be a plan. That plan needs to take into consideration that learner's current proficiency level (including strengths and weaknesses in all language and culture areas), learning styles, personal interests and needs, nature of aptitude, and realistic opportunities for learning, along with a clear understanding of the linguistic and cultural peculiarities of the language being studied that set the teaching of it apart from the teaching of other languages. This assessment requires the teacher to set aside platitudes that are commonly held in today's language-teaching field. It requires the teacher to set aside personal learning preferences and experiences, understanding that "what works for me" may not be "what works for my learner." It requires the teacher to experiment, to replace "should" with "what if," and to be receptive to new or at least different ways of teaching.

Learning plans, however, are not one-shot deals. Once established, typically together with the learner, they need to be revised periodically as learners' proficiency increases, learning opportunities change, and personal interests move in new directions. The learning plan is not a destination; it is a road map and, as such, a working document.

Further Reading

Al-Khanji, Rajai Rasheed, Brendel, Gerd, Hoskins, Vicki, & Jasser, Amal. Pending. *Achieving Native-Like Second-Language Proficiency: A Catalogue of Critical Factors: Volume 2: Writing.* SJB, CA: MSI Press.

Belcher, Diane and Connor, Uhl. 2001. *Reflections on Multiliterate Lives.* The Hague: Multilingual Matters.

Brendel, Gerd, Degueldre, Christian, & Sarraj, Inas. 2005. "How I Reached High-Level Proficiency in ESL: The Personal Odysseys of *Distinguished Language Journal* Abstractors/ Translators." *Journal for Distinguished Language Studies 3*: 5-8.

Byrnes, Heidi. 2002. "Toward Academic-Level Foreign-Language Abilities: Reconsidering Foundational Assumptions, Expanding Pedagogical Options." In *Developing Professional-Level Language Proficiency* (Leaver & Shekhtman, eds.). Cambridge, UK: Cambridge University Press.

Cole, Charles, & Atwell, Sabine. 2004. "Two Experiences, Two Paths to Language Proficiency: An Unintentional Debate." *Journal for Distinguished Language Proficiency 2*: 5-10.

Dubinsky, Inna, Glad, John, Riley, Maureen, & Robin, Richard. 2004. "Kruglyj stol po voprosam dostizhenija chertvertogo urovnja vladenija russkim razgovornym jazykom." *Teaching and Learning to Near-Native Levels of Language Proficiency: The Proceedings of the Spring and Fall 2003 Conferences of the Coalition of Distinguished Language Center*s (Leaver & Shekhtman, eds.). Salinas, CA: MSI Press.

Ehrman, Madeline. 1993. "Ego Boundaries and Tolerance of Ambiguity in Second Language Learning." In *Affect in Language Learning.*

Ehrman, Madeline. 1999. "Ego Boundaries Revisited: Toward a Model of Personality and Learning." In *Strategic Interaction and Language Acquisition: Theory, Practice, and Research* (Alatis). Washington, DC: Georgetown University Press.

Ehrman, Madeline E., Leaver, Betty Lou, & Oxford Rebecca L. 2003. "A Brief Overview of Individual Differences in Second Language Learning." *System* 31(3): 313-330.

Ehrman, Madeline. 1994. "Weakest and Strongest Learners in Intensive Language Training: A Study of Extremes." In *Faces in a Crowd: Individual Learners in Multisection Programs* (Klee, ed.). Boston: Heinle & Heinle.

Ehrman, Batlay, Romanova, Schramm, & Wei. 2004. "Paths to Native-Like Proficiency: Personalized Experiences in English." In *Teaching and Learning to Near-Native Levels of Second Language Acquisition: Proceedings of the Spring and Fall 2003 Conferences of the Coalition of Distinguished Language Centers* (Leaver & Shekhtman, eds.). Salinas, CA: MSI Press.

Fisher, Patricia. 2004. "Mesa redonda sobre la adquisición del nivel de competencia 4 en español." *Teaching and Learning to Near-Native Levels of Language Proficiency: The Proceedings of the Spring and Fall 2003 Conferences of the Coalition of Distinguished Language Centers* (Leaver & Shekhtman, eds.). Salinas, CA: MSI Press.

Hartman, Ernest. 1991. *Boundaries in the Mind.* NY: Basic Books.

Leaver, Betty Lou. 2001. "Is Teaching Russian Really Different from Teaching Other Foreign Languages?" *ACTR Letter 28* (2), 1-5.

Leaver, Betty Lou. 2003. *Individualized Learning Plans for Very Advanced Learners of Foreign Language.* Salinas, CA: MSI Press.

Leaver, Betty Lou. 2004. "Developing Individualized Study Plans for Lifelong Learning" In *Teaching and Learning to Near-Native Levels of Language Proficiency: The Proceedings of the Spring and Fall 2003 Conferences of the Coalition of Distinguished Language Centers* (Leaver & Shekhtman, eds.). Salinas, CA: MSI Press.

Leaver, Betty Lou. 2004. "Interviews with High-Level Speakers: Surprises in the Data." *Journal for Distinguished Language Studies* 2: 27-40.

Leaver, Betty Lou, & Atwell, Sabine. 2002. "Preliminary Qualitative Findings from a Study of the Processes Leading to the Advanced Professional Proficiency Level (ILR 4)" In *Developing Professional-Level Language Proficiency* (Leaver & Shekhtman, eds.). Cambridge, UK: Cambridge University Press.

Leaver, Betty Lou, Rifkin, Benjamin, & Shekhtman, Boris, with Banner, Chaput, Evans-Romaine, Davidson, Ervin, Garza, Kagan, Lekić, Martin, Miller, Morris, Robin, and Zaitsev. 2004. "Apples and Oranges Are Both Fruit, But They Don't Taste the Same: A Response to Wong and Van Patten." *Foreign Language Annals 37* (1): 125-132.

2

Be Sensitive to Learning Styles

Betty Lou Leaver
(Defense Language Institute Foreign Language Center)

Madeline Ehrman
(Foreign Service Institute)

Teachers working with language learners at all levels have for some decades now recognized that learners have specific sensory and cognitive preferences when it comes to learning and specific ways of interacting with classmates. These individual differences can be very important both in positive and negative ways in the language process, the significance of which may change as one progresses up the ladder of proficiency.

One phenomenon that has been observed by language teachers and their learners over time is the "tortoise and hare" syndrome. Learners who are painfully accurate—and therefore slow— in the beginning of language study often outdistance their faster peers who can plateau at the Advanced/Superior threshold because they have become comfortable with being "awfully fluent."

What is clear to teachers of high-level learners and to learners themselves is that language and communication depend upon many variables. It is not enough to be a good reader (as visual learners usually are) or a good listener (as auditory learners usually are). A high-level language user must be a good reader *and* a good listener, regardless of sensory preference.

In the same way, it is not enough to be fluent (as most synoptic learners are) or accurate (as most ectenic learners are). One must be both fluent and accurate. It is not enough to see the underlying patterns (as levelers do) or to notice the fine structural, cultural, behavioral, and sociolinguistic differences (as sharpeners do). One must both level and sharpen, i.e., both see the patterns *and* see the differences. Both sides of the brain are used in native language. Both sides of the brain are needed for native-like language use.

The research is not complete and not conclusive about which learning styles are most conducive to achieve high levels of language proficiency, and certainly learners of all learning styles and personality types can benefit from the incorporation of learner variables such as cognitive styles and personality types into the learning process and their individualized learning plans. However, one aspect of high-level language learning stands out clearly: learners must learn to style-flex if they want to achieve native-like proficiency for a wide range of (opposing) learning styles are needed for acquiring language at this level. The wise teacher, then, not only adapts lesson plans to learner learning styles but also teaches learning strategies associated with the opposing learning styles and creates activities which require the learner to style-flex on an increasingly frequent basis.

For example, synoptic learners who are often cavalier about making slips of the tongue even in their own language can be led to greater accuracy through targeted amounts of old-fashioned drilling, more natural opportunities for repetition, awareness awakening (e.g., reacting very strongly when a synoptic learner mis-speaks), and monitor development through repeated tape-recording and mistake-finding. Ectenic learners can be led to a stronger "feel" for the language through etymology activities, work with roots, and semantic mapping—activities that allow them to use their well-honed analytic skills at the same time as they are developing the ability to level differences in order to find the patterns that define the nature of the language.

The kind of activities needed for each learner will vary, depending on his or her learning style profile. Every profile is different, and therein lies the challenge and the fun of teaching learners at this— and any—proficiency level. The additional excitement in teaching learners at the highest levels of language proficiency is not the challenge of adapting materials and learning activities to learners' learning styles but in adapting learners to the learning styles required by the materials and real-life activities that near-native language users must be able to handle.

Further Reading

Ehrman, Madeline E., & Leaver, Betty Lou. (2002). *The E&L Cognitive Styles Construct*. Unpublished, copyrighted, and registered instrument.

Ehrman, Madeline E., & Leaver, Betty Lou. 2003. "Cognitive Styles in the Service of Language Learning." *System 31* (3): 393-415.

Jackson, Frederick. 2004. "Observations on Training Beyond-3 in an Institutional Setting." In *Teaching and Learning to Near-Native Levels of Second Language Acquisition: Proceedings of the Spring and Fall 2003 Conferences of the Coalition of Distinguished Language Centers* (Leaver & Shekhtman, eds.). Salinas, CA: MSI Press.

Leaver, Betty Lou. 1986. "Hemisphericity of the Brain and Foreign Language Teaching." *Folia Slavica* 8:1, pp. 76-90.

Leaver, Betty Lou. 2019. *Think Yourself into Becoming a Language Learning Super Star*. Hollister: MSI Press.

Leaver, Betty Lou, Dubinsky, Inna, & Champine, Melina. 2004. *Passport to the World: Learning to Communicate in a Foreign Language*. San Diego, CA: LARC Press.

Leaver, Betty Lou. Forthcoming. *The E&L Cognitive Style Construct: Supercharging Language Learning One Mind at a Time*. Hollister, CA: MSI Press.

Shekhtman, Boris, Leaver, Betty Lou, & Ehrman, Madeline E. 2004. "Questions Typically Asked by Learners in Level 4 Classrooms." In *Teaching and Learning to Near-Native Levels of Second Language Acquisition: Proceedings of the Spring and Fall 2003 Conferences of the Coalition of Distinguished Language Centers* (Leaver & Shekhtman). Salinas, CA: MSI Press.

3

Treat Learners as Peers with Different Personality Types

Madeline Ehrman
(Foreign Service Institute)

The first thing that most teachers of high-level proficiency courses notice about their learners is that they are not babes in the woods waiting to be led along the path to their destination. Just the opposite. They are experienced language learners.[3] They know what has worked and has not worked for them. They know what their learning needs are, and they know what their

---

[3] The term, *expert language learner*, likely first introduced by Richard Brecht and Ronald Walton for a series of research projects on the expertise of language learners embracing a third language conducted at the Defense Language Institute by them, Victor Frankl, Maria Lekić, and William Rivers and at the time as "learners with sufficient experience at language learning and sufficient awareness of that experience to make conscious use of it in their third-language courses" (Rivers, 1996, p. 4) and has been subsequently further used in the language-teaching profession to refer in general to learners who have learned more than one language and are skilled at language acquisition. More often than not, this nomenclature refers to language learners with lower levels of proficiency in two or more languages and good grades in their language courses. The expert language learner we are referring to here may be a polyglot (high-level proficiency in two or more languages) but may as well be someone who has gained Advanced Professional Proficiency in just one language. The expertise is not in picking up languages quickly at the beginning of language study but in methodical and successful acquisition of language to very high levels. The personalities exhibited by these two different kinds of learners can be immense: low-level expert language learners tend to be eager, impatient, and frustrated by slower classmates whereas high-level expert language learners tend to be demanding, controlling, and self-aware. They require different approaches from their teachers.

destination or goal is. As a result, they are often highly critical of their teachers, and some very good teachers have found teaching courses at the highest levels of language proficiency to be unnervingly difficult, contrary to the frequent assumption that teaching really capable and accomplished learners should be easy.

Since highly advanced learners bring much to the learning process, including the knowledge of how to learn, of what they want from their learning experience, and of what they presume to be good and poor methods of teaching, the most successful instructors at this level are ones who go *with* the flow, not against it. In most cases step one is to determine what learner expectations are.

Of course, the experienced Level-4 teacher is more knowledgeable about the learning process than the learner, even if the learner thinks otherwise. Step two becomes a negotiating and awareness-development process through which the teacher discusses the learner's goals, strengths, and weaknesses and possible learning plans that[4] will take advantage of the learners' strengths and shore up his/her weaknesses in order to reach the specific goal.

In addition to expectations resulting from previous learning, learner personality types[5] can play an important role

---

[4] The personality types described in this and subsequent paragraphs are those proposed by Carl Jung (1921) and systematized in the Western world by the mother-daughter team of Katherine Briggs and Isabella Briggs Myers in their Myers Briggs Type Indicator (MBTI)—note that the MBTI spells extroversion and extraversioni (Briggs Myers & Myers, 1995; Keirsey & Bates, 1988) and in the Eastern world as the "science" of socionics (see Filatova, 2010, for the first English-language book-length publication on the topic of socionics).

[5] The term, *temperament*, has been used by some, most notably Keirsey and Bates (1984); however, the most common term in use is *personality type*. Following this common usage, the direct translation of the term used by Jung (1921) himself, and the desire to avoid a confusion with the widely known and much older proposed categories of Greek temperaments (Rolfe, 2002), this volume uses the term *personality type* in referring to all "styles" emanating from the work of Jung.

in a high-level classroom, one in which their language prowess will allow them to hold sway with the teacher. Thus, extroverted learners will likely want to do a lot of the talking and, if also synoptic in cognition, may not necessarily even notice when corrections are being made. The role of the teacher in this case is to lead the learner from behind, to take notes and correct later, and to help the learner develop an awareness of natural error correction (discussed later). Introverted learners, on the other hand, may want to have the opportunity to prepare in advance before holding forth. Helping them prepare to deliver public lectures in the target language is an excellent way to develop the monologue skills of any learner, but especially of introverts.

Teachers sometimes expect all high-level learners to embrace the culture of the society where the studied language is spoken and to seek out any and all opportunities to interact with native speakers. This, however, is not the attitude of all successful language users. Intuitive-Feelers are more likely to meet this expectation than other personality groups. Intuitive-Thinkers often study language because of their interest in systems and linguistics—and they are quite willing to study the culture from afar. Sometimes, they do not even like the culture of the regions where the language they are studying is spoken. Yet, this has not impeded them from reaching native-like levels of proficiency. The successful instructor of Superior and Distinguished learners respects such differences in personality type and allows learners to acquire knowledge and proficiency, interacting with native speakers in ways that are comfortable for them and typical for their own personality in their own culture. Indeed, the skilled Distinguished-level instructor helps learners to display their own personality traits in culturally appropriate ways such that they come across in the other culture as the same kind of person that they are perceived to be in the native culture.

This is not to say that sometimes teachers do not need to encourage learners to undertake activities that might be uncomfortable because such activities "are good for them" or because it is necessary to change tone, behavior, and/or content of interactions in order for them to project their personality *as it is* in the culture being studied. All learners need to be able to interact with speakers from the foreign culture and to interact both appropriately and in ways that allow them to be in as much control of the interaction as they are in their native language (see later). However, interaction with people of like interest and personality type is not only apt to be more comfortable, it is also apt to be more successful—and in reality, most people, even in their own culture, gravitate toward others with whom they share common experiences, interests, and values.

Further Reading

Briggs Myers Isabella with Peter Myers. 1995. *Gifts Differing.* Palo Alto, CA: Consulting Psychologists Press.

Ehrman, Madeline E. 2002. "The Learner at the Superior-Distinguished Threshold." In *Developing Professional Level Language Proficiency* (Leaver & Shekhtman). Cambridge, UK: Cambridge University Press.

Ehrman, Madeline E. "Teachers and Learners at the Threshold of Four Level Proficiency." *ACTR Letter 28*(3): 1-3.

Filatova, Ekaterina. 2010. Understanding the People around You: An Introduction to Socionics. Hollister, CA: MSI Press.

Jung, Carl G. 1921. *Psychologishe Typen.* Zurich: Rascher Verlag.

Keirsey, David, & Bates, Marilyn. 1984. *Please Understand Me: Character and Temperament Types.* Del Mar, CA: Prometheus Press.

Rivers, William P. 1996. "Self-Directed Language Learner and Third-Language Learner. ERIC Document 411 679.

Rolfe, Randy. 2002. The Four Temperaments: A Rediscovery the Ancient Way of Understanding Health and Character. Boston: Da Capo Press.

Rubin, Joan. 2005. "The Expert Language Learner: A Review of Good Language Learner Studies and Learning Strategies." In *Expertise in Second Language Learning and Teaching* (Johnson). London, UK: Springer.

Shekhtman, Boris. 2003. *Working with Advanced Language Learners.* Salinas CA: MSI Press.

Thomas Jesús Garza, Ed. D.

#4

Promote Learner Autonomy

Kenneth Shepard
(Colleges of Technology in Oman)

Generating individualized learning plans, conducting diagnostic assessments, and understanding learners' learning styles and personality types, especially the behaviors of expert language learners, are the underpinnings needed to promote learner autonomy. If any one characteristic of the learning process *is* common to all high-level language learners, it is that the process is neither short nor contained exclusively in the classroom. There will be many times, experiences, and opportunities in which the learner will be swimming in the ocean of language without a lifeguard nearby. The teacher's role, then, beyond teaching the learner to be a good swimmer, is to help the learner develop flotation devices for when he or she gets in trouble.

Some flotation devices are communication strategies for dealing with and learning from new language and culture input, such as knowing how to ask questions about cultural in culturally appropriate ways, knowing how to change the topic of a conversation deftly, and knowing when and how to excuse oneself appropriate from a conversation or group interaction. Practicing such communication strategies in the classroom can be very helpful in making them resources that are automatically recalled when needed.

Other flotation devices are strategies for controlling automatic negative responses. When finding themselves on *terra incognita*, even the best language users can flounder from momentary confusion, self-doubt, and discomfort. Teachers can emotion-proof their highly proficient learners for such situations by creating possible scenarios in the classroom and in the émigré community; in so doing, they can not only provide support, they can also help learners develop personalized strategies for dealing with awkward and other difficult-to-manage situations. Teachers can also help learners get started in keeping diaries of their observations of their own interactions in social and formal environments, using the diary as an outlet for releasing the emotions associated with the experience.

More than having survival and growth skills, however, learners at the Superior level who are trying to reach near-native levels of proficiency need to know how to continue learning without teacher support. They need to understand the learning process. They need to be able to put together their own individualized learning plans and modify them as circumstances change. They need to know where to find learning opportunities and learning materials.

Becoming self-directed is often less a matter of personality and persuasion than of knowledge and resources. Teachers who send learners out to do research and find materials on their own, rather than hand feeding them, are helping them to build lifelong learning strategies. Teachers who provide them with an understanding of how learning happens (or does not) and how they can facilitate their own learning are providing them with more lifelong learning strategies. And teachers who help them understand what differing kinds of learning opportunities can do for them and show them where to find them or how to set them up are, indeed, preparing the lifelong learner for success.

Further Reading

Cohen, Bella. 2020. *Diagnostic Assessment at the Superior/ Distinguished Threshold*. Hollister, CA: MSI Press.

Leaver, Ehrman, and Shekhtman. 2005. *Achieving Success in Second Language Acquisition* Cambridge University Press.

Leaver, Betty Lou. 2003. *Individualized Study Plans for Very Advanced Learners of Foreign Languages*. Hollister, CA: MSI Press.

Little, David. 2021. "Language Learning Autonomy and Transformative Classroom Practice." In *Transformative Language Learning and Teaching* (Leaver, Davidson, & Campbell). Cambridge, UK: Cambridge University Press.

Scharle, Szabo, and Ur. 2000. *Learner Autonomy: A Guide to Developing Learner Responsibility* Cambridge University Press,).

Cotterall. 1999. *Learner Autonomy in Language Learning: Defining the Field and Effecting Change.* Peter Lang Publishing.

Wenden. 1991. *Learner Strategies for Learner* Autonomy. Prentice Hall.

5

Develop Learners' Control
of Self-Expression

Gerd Brendel
(Defense Language Institute Foreign Language Center)

Tailoring one's language to one's audience and purpose of communicating through speaking or writing in the first place is considered one of the hallmarks of the Distinguished level of language proficiency. In our native language we have learned through upbringing and education, more or less successfully, to adjust our language register to the person we are addressing.

We address a friend differently from how we address the mayor of our town unless she is a personal friend and the conversation takes place in an informal setting like at a mutual friend's barbecue. If the purpose of our conversation is intended to maintain harmonious social relations with the mayor as a friend, we will in all likelihood engage in informal small talk about our families, hobbies mutual friends and the like in a familiar, if not chummy or intimate tone depending on how well we know our conversational partner. If the purpose of our talk with the mayor is official like a neighborhood petition to increase police patrols at night, we will automatically speak in a formal register. We would assume a friendly and courteous stance that maintains emotional distance to our interlocutor. In this kind of formal situation where we petition an official with a well-considered and supported request, we would choose our words deliberately avoiding all slang and vulgar colloquial expressions.

As finding the appropriate register requires deliberation of our choice of words, attention to correct grammar usage as well as thoughtful consideration of the organization of our intentions and ideas, writing practice offers an effective way to learn to control one's self-expression because writing, as opposed to spontaneous speech, allows time for such careful planning at the word, sentence, paragraph, and discourse level. Moreover, word-processing programs provide writers efficient help in planning, drafting, revising, and final editing of a text.

My learners of German as a world language, for example, enjoyed answering personal ads in the classified sections of German local newspapers. These ads provided them with the opportunity to practice the familiar register connecting them in a very personal, but socio-culturally appropriate way to the person who had placed the ad. Writing letters to the editor in response to articles in the opinion and editorial sections of national German newspapers that my learners found particularly controversial was another motivating activity to practice their control of the appropriate register. In this instance, they worked on developing their control of the formal register with all of its requirements of being well thought out, appropriately worded, respectful in tone, yet persistent in supporting one's argument counter to the opinion advocated in the article they were responding to.

Some of my learners were interested in learning how to give public speeches. I would provide them with high-level models that are available from the Department of Rhetoric at the University of Tuebingen as the best German speeches of the year. The department's web-site (www.uni-tuebingen.de/uni/nas) provides the printed text of the selected speeches as well as commentaries and explanations why these speeches were selected as prime examples of excellence in public speaking. Learners were tasked to use the original speeches as much as possible and substitute the German specific content with content from their native country and culture. Learners would then rewrite speeches like those by authors Rolf Hochuth on the deleterious influence of English on contemporary German or Martin Walser on the undue influence of public opinion through the media on an individual's freedom of expression.

I also used this collection of speeches for structured learner practice in rewriting particularly complex thoughts expressed in some passages of these speeches in a less formal register. I would frame these tasks in simple scenarios asking learners to recapture the meaning of the selected passages in their own words in a letter to a good friend.

Only the number of interesting models that teachers can find limits variations of these rewriting tasks from very formal to informal and vice versa and they are sure to develop learners' self-expression in a range of registers from the intimate and chummy to the highly formal.

Further Reading

Brauer, Gerd. 2001. *Pedagogy of Language Learning in Higher Education: An Introduction.* Ablex Publishing.

McKay, Sandra Lee and Nancy H. Hornberger, eds. 1995. *Sociolinguistics and Language Teaching.* London: Cambridge University Press.

Pachler, Norbert, ed. 1999. *Teaching Modern Foreign Languages at Advanced Level.* London: Routledge.

Willis, Jane, Peter Eldin, and Angela Lansbury. 2003. *The Complete Speechmaker.* UK: Cassell Ltd.

6

Build an Understanding of Genre

Frederick Jackson
(National Foreign Language Center)

The use of public speeches mentioned in earlier in developing learners' range of self-expression through the gamut of familiar and informal to formal and highly rhetorical registers is one example of building an understanding of genre and developing writing skills by rewriting speeches with different content and in different registers. For purposes of developing a rhetorically effective style, I suggest having learners copy selected model texts by rewriting them from their own point of view and with their own content.

There will, obviously, be individual issues like stylistic schemata prevalent in the learners' L1, but not in the target L2. American learners learning German, for example, will discover that their school standard of writing as concisely and precisely as possible is not a German academic virtue. More often than not, the American standard of keeping one's academic prose short and simple is replaced in German by its opposite of keeping one's writing long and complex as a badge of honor of the writer's standing as an academician and intellectual. Learners will develop this kind of German style by copying long-winded German models but making them their own by rewriting the models from their own perspective and relating their own content.

Other activities that help develop learners' genre competencies include rewriting texts from one genre into another. For example, have learners render an interview into an objective third person report. This task gets to be a quite challenging if the interview is laden with emotions. Another task for developing learners understanding and control of genre would be to retell a comic story in a narrative that reflects as fully as possible the original's implications and allusions. Another useful exercise would be to have learners rewrite a highly technical text in their field of expertise for a popular magazine and its general readership. What recommends these types of rewriting tasks is their strict focus on genres and their typical organizational forms (report, interview, narrative, technical vs. general audience reports etc.) and their intensive practice of writing giving credence to the insight that writing is best developed through writing.

Further Reading

Byrnes. Heidi, Heather D. Heger-Guntharp, and Katharine Sprang, eds. 2006. *Educating for Advanced Foreign Language Capacities.* Washington, D.C.: Georgetown University Press.

Di Vito, Nadine O'Connor. 1997. *Patterns across Spoken and Written French: Empirical Research on the Interaction among Forms, Function, and Genres.* Boston: D. C. Heath.

Huettner, Julia Isabel. 2007. *Academic Language in a Foreign Language: An Extended Genre Analysis of Learner Texts.* Peter Lang Publishing.

Paltridge, Brian Richard. 2001. *Genre and the Language Learning Classroom.* Ann Arbor, MI: University of Michigan Press.

7

Develop Learner Independence

Peter Glanville
(University of Maryland)

Second language learners who reach Superior proficiency have typically developed a high degree of learner independence along the way, characterized by a set of practices and behaviors that allow them to operate in an educational setting as an active partner in the learning process rather than a passive consumer. Some learners appear to be relatively independent innately, but second language teachers can benefit larger numbers of learners by providing explicit strategy training to move them along the continuum of from dependence, to independence, and potentially to full autonomy. Dependent learners rely on textbooks and teachers for vocabulary, grammar instruction, and error correction. Their interaction with texts is structured around comprehension exercises that require correct answers, where the teacher or textbook writer has determined what is important in a text and what the learner should draw from it. A shift to independence comes when learners begin to notice new language in the input they experience and to document and then activate it in their own linguistic production. Independent learners monitor their own language use and self-correct and set goals for improvement. When they process texts, they identify problems in their comprehension, and have strategies and procedures for working to solve them. Learners with these skills are well placed to reach the Superior level of proficiency and to continue improving or maintaining their language level as fully autonomous learners when they leave formal language instruction, whether that be for the workplace, for education in another field, for fieldwork overseas, or to serve as educators themselves.

Teachers can encourage independent learning by focusing on how learners are learning in the foreign-language classroom: how they are building their vocabulary, their idiomatic expressions, and their ability to switch between language registers and employ different discourse patterns; how they formulate, check, and reformulate hypotheses when processing texts; and how they approach and monitor their spoken and written production. This process involves assigning tasks that reward learners for the processes and procedures they employ to complete them and for how these change or improve over time–in other words, for the documentation of independent skill development.

For reading and listening, learners can be explicitly instructed to write down the main idea of a text and to provide some supporting details. They can be asked to identify an area of the text where their comprehension breaks down and to write down what they think it might be saying and then to check this guess by looking up problem words in a dictionary, analyzing grammatical structures, determining the referents of pronouns and so on, before writing down an improved interpretation. Following this, they might note any new language that they would like to incorporate into their own linguistic repertoire. Such assignments provide learners with a degree of freedom to focus on what is salient and accessible to them in a text—what they can do rather than what they cannot. They are inherently motivating since learners identify and solve their own comprehension problems, and there is always a language gain because they extract useful language to be used in their subsequent speaking and writing. In completing these assignments, learners develop the habit of reading and listening for meaning while also analyzing the language used to construe it.

Production tasks can move learners toward the fluency, complexity, and accuracy characteristic of the Superior level of proficiency by requiring them to plan out not just what they will say but also how they will say it. Assignments where learners record a response to a prompt can be accompanied by instructions asking them to produce a short, bulleted outline in English of what they want to say and to insert the foreign language items that they would like to activate during the recording into the appropriate place in the outline. These may be vocabulary items arising from the learner's interactions with texts, grammatical structures, expressions, or whatever the learner would like to further cement his or her ability to recall and use in the future. The outline is submitted together with the recording. The aim here is that when recording, fluency is improved because the response is already considered and planned out, while complexity is increased as the learner activates new language with each assignment. Accuracy is targeted by requiring the learner to listen to and correct the recording before submission, either by overwriting errors on the recording itself, or by submitting a list of errors and their corrections. A similar procedure may be followed for writing assignments, where at least part of the grade comes from planning out language use and selecting new language for activation, in addition to incorporating teacher feedback from previous drafts. Through these assignments, learners develop the habit of deliberately activating the language that they have noticed around them, and an understanding of the importance of creating contexts in which to do so. Planned speech gives them the time to do this that spontaneous speech does not. Where they might avoid using a complex grammatical structure or a lexical item that they have not fully gained control over in spontaneous speech, planned speech assignments specifically require them to do this. In follow-up class activities, dialogue on similar topics provides an opportunity for learners to reproduce elements of their planned speech or their writing more spontaneously as they engage in class discussion.

Superior-level learners, of course, already exhibit the ability to identify and solve comprehension problems and to exploit texts as linguistic resources by extracting and using new language. This raises the question of how many of them reached Superior because it occurred to them to do this and how many were explicitly trained to do so. Teachers who seek to increase the number of learners reaching Superior proficiency in their languages might do well to consider focusing on learner independence as a means to provide learners with the skills it takes to get there.

Further Reading

Benson, Phil, & Voller, Peter. 1997. *Autonomy and Independence in Language Learning.* London and New York: Longman.

Griffiths, Carol. 2008, "Strategies and Good Language Learners." In *Lessons from Good Language Learners* (Griffiths). Cambridge: Cambridge University Press.

Holec, Henri. 1981, *Autonomy in Foreign Language Learning.* Oxford: Pergamon.

Oxford, Rebecca L., & Leaver, Betty Lou. 1996. A synthesis of strategy instruction for language learners. In R. Oxford (ed.) *Language Learning Strategies Around the World: Cross-cultural Perspectives* (pp. 227-246). Manoa: University of Hawai'i Press.

Rowsell, Leona V., & Libben, Gary. 1994. "The Sound of One Hand Clapping: How to Succeed in Independent Language Learning." *Canadian Modern Language Review* 50 (4), 668-688.

Rubin, Joan. 1975. What the "Good Language Learner" Can Teach Us. *TESOL Quarterly* 9 (1), 41-51.

Schumann, John. 2001. "Learning as Foraging." In (eds) *Motivation and Second Language Acquisition* (Dörnyei & Schmidt). Manoa: University of Hawai'i Press.

Wenden, Anita L. 1991. *Learner Strategies for Learner Autonomy*. Hemel Hempstead, UK: Prentice Hall.

Section II

Focus on Instruction

8

Develop Memory

Betty Lou Leaver
(Defense Language Institute Foreign Language Center)

Svetlana Sibrina
(The George Washington University)

Boris Shekhtman
(Specialized Language Training Center)

Language learners and teachers, especially those working at high levels of proficiency, know that a memory is key to mastering a language. Teachers at high levels of language proficiency are therefore faced with the task of helping learners to further develop their memory, especially memory for language features. Teachers who have focused on this aspect of high-level language development have, fortunately, found instruments to make learners' memorization process more effective. Three of these are grammar formularization, memorization techniques, and adaptation to cognitive style.

Grammar formularization is the practice of turning variations into singularities, the complex into the simple, many elements into few. In other words, the grammar is distilled by the teacher to the barest of its component parts. Grammar formularization reduces the cognitive load on the learner when dealing with new information, and, therefore, the amount of material that learners can memorize increases geometrically. Even the contracted forms of language, irregularities, and exceptions can be shown to adhere to one or another more general formula, which is crucial for Superior-level learners as they attempt to internalize the underlying linguistic code of the language—the same code that the native speaker internalizes in early childhood.

The second instrument, memorization techniques, involves a variety of exercises that focus on internalization of structure and lexicon. Such exercises can be repetitions, lexical and grammatical substitution drills, requiring learners to ask questions based on a memorized model, requiring learners to use newly presented models in meaningful speech, putting selected materials on "memorization cards," mixing difficult-to-remember units in with easy-to-remember ones, making learners responsible for identifying and tracking their own mistakes, requiring learners to use the target pattern after being presented with a symbol, slowing down learners' speech so that they have time to control possible mistakes, color- coding new lexical and grammatical features, emotionally charging the classroom during exercises that require memorization, and the purposeful and frequent use of difficult-to-remember grammar features and lexical items in routine communication at times when work on the items in question is not occurring, among a wide variety of other exercises. Such exercises, of course, can be used at any level of instruction; the difference is that at high levels, the complexity and scope of utterances take on a sophistication nearly equivalent to that used by the native speaker.

The teacher's knowledge of learners' learning styles and personality types and understanding of how these styles promote or impede memorization can help teachers individualize input and practice, making the exercises more efficient. Making sure to start with the big picture before working on details can facilitate the memorization of the information by synoptic learners (those who learn holistically, in top-down ways), just as attention to the details prior to trying to cope with the big picture will help ectenic learners (those who learn atomistically, in bottom-up ways) (see Ehrman, Leaver, & Oxford, 2003, for a greater exploration of learning styles, especially the synoptic-ectenic distinctions proposed by Ehrman and Leaver [2003]). Extroverts generally prefer memorization activities that involve groups of learners whereas introverts prefer to work alone. Other personality variables can affect memorization effectiveness as well, e.g., intuitive thinkers (NT) will seek out a logical system behind grammatical expressions and be able to accept anomalies as interesting deviations whereas sensing thinkers often become frustrated by grammatical irregularities.[6] Since there are many different learning styles and personality types, any of which can be very important (or not important at all) to the learning process of any given learner, the teacher at high levels of language proficiency is, once again, first and foremost an analyst, who uses information gleaned from observation to tailor instruction to each individual learner.

Success in learning a language depends not only on presentation of the material and teachers' experience but also on the learners' personal efforts to memorize this material. Learners' efforts can be significantly aided by two things: an awareness of their own learning style (i.e., knowledge of how thy learn and remember best) and the effective use of mnemonic devices. Both of these things can be taught to them by teachers who are focused on individualization.

Further Reading

Anon. December 16, 2002. "For a Good Memory, Try Harder." *The Washington Post.*

---

[6] A large number of books and articles on personality type in the language classroom have appeared during and since the 1990s, many of them prompted by the research of Madeline Ehrman (1990a, 1990b, 1996). At least two weeks have moved beyond the learner as an individual within a classroom and have examined the interpersonal and intraclass dynamics manifesting themselves in overt and covert ways within a classroom (Dabbs and Leaver, 2019; Ehrman and Dornyei, 1998).

Dabbs, Laura, & Leaver, Betty Lou. 2019. *The Invisible Foreign Language Classroom: Bringing Hidden Dynamics to Light for Individual and Group Success*. Hollister, CA: MSI Press.

Ehrman, Madeline E. 1990a. "Owls and Doves: Cognition, Personality, and Learning Success." In *Linguistics, Language Teaching and Language Acquisition: The interdependence of Theory, Practice, and Research* (Alatis). Washington DC: Georgetown University Press.

Ehrman, Madeline E. 1990b. "The Role of Personality Type in Adult Language Learning: An Ongoing Investigation. In *Language Aptitude Reconsidered* (Parry & Stansfield). Englewood Cliffs NJ: Prentice Hall.

Ehrman, Madeline E. 1993. "The Type Differentiation Indicator and Foreign Language Learning." In *Conscious Choices, Unconscious Forces: Implications of Type, Temperament, and the MBTI* (Robinson). Kansas City MO: Association for Psychological Type.

Ehrman, M. E. 1996, *Understanding Second Language Learning Difficulties*. Thousand Oaks, CA: Sage.

Ehrman, Madeline E., & Leaver, Betty Lou. 2002. "Cognitive styles in the service of language learning." *System* 31: 393-415.

Ehrman, Madeline E., Leaver, Betty Lou, & Oxford, Rebecca L. 2003. "A Brief Overview of Individual Differences in Second Language Learning. *System* 31: 313-329.

Ehrman, Madeline E., & Dörnyei, Zoltán. Interpersonal Dynamics in Second Language Education: The Visible and Invisible Classroom.

Leaver, Echo E. 1999. "Making the Most of Memory." In *Passport to the World: Learning to Communicate in a Foreign Language* (Leaver, Dubinsky, & Champine). San Diego, CA: LARC Press.

Miller. 1956. "The Magical Number Seven, Plus or Minus Two: Some Limits on Our Capacity for Processing Information." *The Psychological Review 63*: 81-97.

Piaget & Inhelder. 1973. *Memory and Intelligence.* Basic Books. Shekhtman, Boris. 2003. *Working with Advanced Foreign Language Learners.* MSI Press.

Terrell, Tracy. 1976. "Acquisition in the Natural Approach: The Binding/Access Framework." *Modern Language Journal 70* (3): 63-76.

Thomas Jesús Garza, Ed. D.

9

Develop Learners' Capacity for Sophisticated Forms of Communication

Boris Shekhtman
(Specialized Language Training Center)

Natalia Lord
(Foreign Service Institute)

Superior-level learners should have complete command of typical monologues and dialogues, so, to move upward in proficiency, Distinguished-level learners must develop control over more profound and professionally crucial forms of communicative competence. While learners are able to control some of these forms at lower levels of proficiency, the Level-4 professional language user must be able to select and use nearly all of these in much the same way as an educated native speaker, without resorting to compensation strategies. The tasks that such learners can expect to be taught by language instructors to accomplish this level of effective command of communication typically include the following:

- Problem-solving discussion (situations)
- Interpreting language and culture
- Interview
- Briefing
- Formal presentation Debate
- Negotiation

Problem-solving discussion. The professional working overseas regularly faces situations in which s/he needs high-level language skills to solve specific problems. A businessman closing a deal, for example, needs to meet with his/her counterparts to discuss a myriad of specific details concerning the transaction from transportation, delivery and storage issues, questions concerning insurance, security arrangements, price, payment schedule and credit issues, etc. Although the services of an interpreter may be available, experience has shown that better results are obtained when the representative of the firm conducts the discussion personally in the target language. In most cases, highly precise expression is needed in order not to create new problems caused by misinterpretation of words while trying to solve current problems. Since these sorts of discussions are closely to related to the learners' current or future work, teachers typically ask learners to bring real problems to class in order to build tasks and exercises around "the real McCoy."

Interpreting language and culture. For many American professionals working in a foreign country, informal interpreting is an integral part of the job. Highly proficient speakers need to be able to move comfortably and seamlessly from one language and culture to the other and back again. Their knowledge and use of parallel structures, idiomatic equivalents, and culturally appropriate forms of expression need to be honed. Distinguished-level speakers need to be able to spot a false cognate and to know the subtle distinctions between the way a certain term may be used in two different cultures. While not training to be a professional interpreter, Distinguished-level language professionals need to be able to transition from their native language and culture to the world language and culture of study without lowering the level and sophistication of their speech. Distinguished-level speakers also must interpret beyond words. In many instances, they find themselves in situations in which they must interpret cultural behaviors and values and discuss in detail concepts which are fundamentally different from those of the target culture and make those concepts clear and accessible to the native speaker. There are, of course, a number of individuals who do work as professional interpreters. For them, all the comments made about this skill are applicable. In addition, they need to have a number of other abilities related to correlating two languages and cultures.

Interview. The process of interviewing someone with the goal of obtaining needed information is an important part of many professional jobs. Using the language being studied for obtaininginformation directly is unarguably an advantage. The Level-4 speaker is able to control the interview and the content emanating from it through taking charge linguistically, setting the tone, and displaying a detailed understanding of both world and native cultures so as to be perceived as an equal partner in the conversation. To prepare for professional-level interviews at higher proficiency levels, learners have several needs. These include (1) practice posing questions using complex structures, (2) practice posing these questions rapidly and automatically, (3) strategies for conducting interviews in general, (4) strategies for planning questions in an order that will elicit more information, and (5) automatic control of phrases needed for clarification, for returning someone to a particular topic, and asking for more precise and specific information.

Briefing. A briefing serves as a vehicle for transmitting information. This may require stating involved policies, defining or clarifying positions, presenting complex research findings and the like. The content of a briefing may be highly professional, specialized, and, therefore, complex. Briefings transmit information in large chunks containing specific details. They may outline a sequence of events leading up to a particular problem before offering a possible outline of a multifaceted solution. To deliver successful briefings, learners need to (1) master complex discourse models that promote organizing their briefings in a clear, logical, and cohesive way, (2) learn the sophisticated expressions used by native speakers when structuring a lengthy monologue on a complex theme, (3) analyze the way briefings are usually structured, and (4) practice planning a briefing in the target language. After delivering practice briefings, learners need to analyze them and see what can be improved the next time. They must also prepare to field questions based on their briefing and then practice doing so.

Presentation. In a presentation, the learner conveys detailed, complex, information as in a briefing but also may state a personal or group point of view. A presentation may contain an analysis of differing points of view and ideas or the evolution of a problem examined from primarily the presenter's point of view. There are a number of ways in which teachers can incorporate presentations into learner programs. For example, an in-depth presentation on a professional topic serves as the culmination of a learner's course of study at the Specialized Language Training Center. Working on this project helps the learner acquire the most necessary professional-level vocabulary by providing a context for it. The process of preparing for a final presentation involves theme selection, in-depth discussions on the theme in the target language, gradual writing of the presentation (section by section), practice in answering questions on the theme of the presentation, rehearsal, and delivering the presentation followed by a question-and-answer session. This process also prepares learners for such professional tasks as television appearances abroad that may call for a statement followed by a question-and-answer session.

Debate. The ability of a learner to take an active part in a professional argument in the target language attests to almost native-like proficiency. In preparation for a debate, it is necessary to develop a number of abilities including (1) clearly and succinctly posing a question, (2) expressing one's point of view with clarity and precision, (3) correctly understanding the positions expressed by other participants, (4) objectively restating the position of an opponent, (5) making effective use of factual material during the discussion, and (6) using a wide array of lexically and structurally appropriate discourse devices in order to express agreement or disagreement or to introduce one's position. To develop all of these abilities requires training.

Negotiation. The professional language user is likely to need to conduct formal and/or informal negotiations. The preparation for negotiation involves developing many of the same abilities needed for preparing for debate but may need even greater focus on linguistically and culturally appropriate verification and bargaining techniques. Understanding interpersonal behaviors, knowing sociolinguistic aspects of formal interactions, and familiarity with the expectations for and conduct of negotiations (including values, mindsets, Weltanschauung, and the like) are essential elements of negotiations and represent areas of important learning for the Level-4 learner. Negotiation requires many of the same skills required for several of the previously described oral communication tasks, including problem-solving, discussion, briefing, and debate. Therefore, exercises used to develop these skills contribute to the development of negotiation skills.

Further Reading

Shekhtman, Boris. 2003. *Working with Advanced Foreign Language Students*. Salinas, CA: MSI Press.

Shekhtman, Boris, ed. 2016. *How to Use Your Russian in Communication Effectively*. CreateSpace.

Shekhtman, Boris, Lord, Natalia, & Kuznetsova, Ekaterina. 2003. "Complication Exercises for Raising the Oral Proficiency Level of Highly Advanced Learners." *Journal for Distinguished Language Studies 1* (1): 32-50.

10

Ask Learners to Find Materials and Teach Class

Betty Lou Leaver
(Defense Language Institute Foreign Language Center)

Many approaches have been employed to change learners' traditional role in the classroom. While admittedly defined in disparate and inconsistent ways across time, languages, and teaching methods publications (Brenner, 2021), a "learner centered" approach *usually* means the combination of (1) a focus on learners' needs, which is central to decision making about teaching and learning; and (2) an understanding of the learning process, how the process takes place, and how the learning process can be enhanced for all learners. A learner-centered environment respects learners' opinions, challenges them, explains to them what is expected from them, allows them to control their learning, encourages them to work cooperatively, gives them the opportunity to work with materials that is interesting and relevant to them, invites them to evaluate the teaching standard and methods, and pays individualized attention to their personal learning styles. Asking learners to find learning materials and participate in teaching activities is a good example of making learners at the center of learning.[7]

When working with Superior-level learners, we are endowed with rich resources, not only material resources but also human resources. We can ask advanced learners to help us find appropriate teaching materials, to act as content tutors or teaching assistants, to host class discussions, and to lead class activities. Our learners may come from different academic and professional backgrounds. Their combined knowledge is definitely better than one teacher. We should make best use of learners' expertise. It is true for all learners but working with lower-level learners can be a challenge because their inadequate language proficiency can be a barrier. The language barrier is removed when we work with advanced learners. Advanced learners have the language ability to participate more actively in learning and teaching.

The most obvious advantage of learners selecting teaching materials is relevance and interest. By bringing in materials of their choice, they tell us what they want to learn. Relevance and interest have a marked influence on learners' motivation and emotion. Motivational and emotional factors induce both the quality of thinking and information processing. In other words, learners can, on the one hand, be better learners if they are involved in choosing the learning content. On the other hand, if the content area is defined and learners are assigned the task of finding related materials to a given topic, the process of locating and evaluating materials is a valuable learning experience. They are challenged to get to the right

---

[7] Since the appearance of this article in the earlier edition of this volume, the emergence of Open Architecture Curricular Design as an approach to teaching foreign languages, generally associated with Transformative Language Learning and Teaching, has brought this principle of learner participation in the selection of teaching materials into sharp focus (Campbell, 2021; Corin 2020; Leaver & Campbell, 2015) although this course attribute has not been previously widely embraced as a component of learner-centered instruction, which has traditionally had more active teacher involvement in the classroom (e.g., Nunan, 1988).

sources, find relevant information, and analyze the usefulness and appropriateness of the information. This task demands them to use linguistic, socio-linguistic, cultural, and content knowledge. Such analytical skills are essential for professionals in the real world.

Another advantage of asking learners to select materials is that they bring in diversified perspectives. They help to present a more balanced and comprehensive view. For instance, in 1995 a course on the challenges of globalization was offered to Advanced- and Superior-level learners at the Monterey Institute of International Studies.[8] Learners enrolled in the class came from different academic departments and programs: business management, public administration, international relations, translation, trade policies, environmental policies, etc. Each field of study focuses on certain aspects of globalization. A business major wants to know the most effective way of integrating goods, services, and capital worldwide; an international relations major is interested in discovering how globalization has caused the integration of economic, cultural, political, and social systems across geographical boundaries; whereas a translation major focuses on the role of language in the two aspects of worldwide product distribution through internationalization (enabling the product to be used without language or culture barriers) and localization (translating and enabling the product for a specific locale). When learners were responsible for finding materials for study and selecting topics for discussion, the whole class gained a more comprehensive picture of globalization. In addition to content depth and width, learners were exposed to diversified vocabulary and discourses. As the world moves toward markets or policies that transcend national borders, dialogues among different

[8] This course was offered on a one-time basis, filled with many international students visiting for the summer, and taught by Stephen B. Stryker (California State University at Stanislaus) and Betty Lou Leaver (then at American Global Studies Institute.)

disciplines will have a positive effect on learners' future careers. As we know, complex subject matters usually require more complex language discourses. Learners are provided with authentic and diversified language input, which enhanced their language learning. When they construct meaning from information, experiences, and their own thoughts and beliefs to learn about the complexity of a subject matter, the learning is more effective.

Asking learners to teach a class or lead class activities is another effective way to improve their language ability. To measure the success of learning, we often test whether the learner can create meaningful, coherent representations of knowledge. Teaching gives learners the opportunity to practice how to construct meaningful and coherent representations of knowledge, and how to communicate to an audience effectively. Initially, their presentation may be sketchy in an area, but through class interactions, peer and teacher feedback, their ability to use the language can be refined by filling gaps, resolving inconsistencies, and deepening their understanding of the language and the subject matter. It is also a great opportunity for learners to use strategic thinking in their own approach to learning, reasoning, and problem solving. They have been using many learning strategies unconsciously. Once teach a class, they will encounter various learning preferences and strategies similar or different from theirs. This enables them to learn about new approaches. Most important, though, they are likely to reflect on how they think and learn. Reflection makes them better learners, as they think about how they think, how they learn, how to set reason- able learning or performance goals, how to select appropriate learning strategies, and how to monitor their progress toward learning goals.

In summary, asking learners to find materials and teach class works seamlessly with the principles of a learner-centered approach in world language education. Learners' participation in teaching enables them to express their need and interest, contribute to the knowledge base, work cooperatively with peers, reflect on their own learning and thinking strategies, and polish their language skills.

Further Reading

Brenner, Nicholas. 2021. "What Is Learner-Centered Instruction? A Quantitative Analysis of English Language Teachers' Perspectives." *TESL-EJ* 25(2): 2-22.

Campbell, Christine. 2021. "Open Architecture Curricular Design: A Fundamental Principle of Transformative Language Learning and Teaching." In *Transformative Language Learning and Teaching* (Leaver, Davidson, & Campbell). Cambridge, UK: Cambridge University Press.

Corin, Andrew R. Spring/Summer 2020. "Open Architecture Curriculum and Transformative Language Learning Revisited: Part 1: The Relationships between Open Architecture Curricular Design and Transformative Language Learning." *ACTR Letter* 47(3-4): 1-2, 4.

Corin, Andrew R. Fall 2020. "Open Architecture Curriculum and Transformative Language Learning Revisited: Part 2: Toward a Constrained Definition of OACD." *ACTR Letter* 48(1): 1-2, 4.

Leaver, Betty Lou. 1998. *Teaching the Whole Class*. Dubuque, IA: Kendall Hunt.

Leaver, Betty Lou. 2000. *Методика индивидуализированного обучения иностранным языкам с учетом влияния когнитивных стилей на их усвоение* (The Influence of Learning Styles on Individualized Foreign Language Teaching and Learning). Dissertation, Pushkin Institute, Moscow, Russia.

Nunan, David. 1988. The Learner-Centered Curriculum. Cambridge, UK: Cambridge University Press.

11

Encourage the Use of Models and Native Speakers Rather Than Dictionaries

Boris Shekhtman
(Specialized Language Training Center)

A survey of language learners who had achieved near-native levels of language proficiency revealed that the vast majority of those using language skills in the workplace much preferred to use models of language and native speakers as lexical aids, rather than dictionaries.

The reason for the preference seems obvious: the models show not only words and sample sentences, but many other aspects of language. Among the most important is text organization. One of the least taught aspects of language is text organization.

Native speakers are also a kind of model. Paying attention to how native speakers use language can serve learners in good stead. Nonverbal communication skills can model interpersonal interaction, turn-taking, register, and many other aspects of language. Level-4 language users are typically capable of watching one or more native speakers accomplishing professional tasks and extracting from the observation the kinds of verbal and nonverbal they need for their own language tasks.

When dictionaries were used, two kinds were preferred: monolingual and specialty. Monolingual dictionaries were preferred for most kinds of work because these dictionaries did a better job of providing nuance and examples of the words in their common usage. In cases of specialty needs, such as engineering or medical terminology, world language users frequently turned to bilingual editions where such were available.

Further Reading

Leaver, Betty Lou. 2003. *Achieving Nativelike Second Language Proficiency: A Catalogue of Critical Factors: Volume 1: Speaking.* Salinas, CA: MSI Press.

Leaver, Betty Lou, Ehrman, Madeline, & Shekhtman, Boris. 2005. *Achieving Success in Second Language Acquisition.* Cambridge, UK: Cambridge University Press.

12

Create Appropriate Study Abroad
Programs for Higher Levels

Dan E. Davidson
(Bryn Mawr College)

Maria D. Lekič
(University of Maryland)

It has long been assumed that the combination of immersion in the native speech community, combined with formal learning, creates the best environment for learning a world language. In a study abroad environment, the key to success is to make learners utilize the rich language resources out of the language classroom. Most study abroad programs generally consist of a curriculum for formal language learning, some cultural excursions–including field trips, field research, or sightseeing trips, some type of living arrangements, optional or required learning through work or service, such as internships and volunteering in local communities, and various forms of learner training. To make the study abroad experience worthwhile, each component should add value to the other components and to the overall experience.

The design of a study abroad program is determined by a multitude of complex interrelations. Most language educators believe that a total immersion is most ideal for language acquisition as learners are exposed to the rich linguistic environment. In practice, the degree of immersion varies among programs. Many conditions hinder programs from being totally immersed into the local culture and community, such as the host country's government policies toward foreigners, the willingness and flexibility of the host institutions to accommodate the linguistic and academic needs of foreign learners, the linguistic, cultural, and psychological preparedness of the learners, learners' motivation, and so on. We can use the "study abroad" experience of international learners in the US to mirror American learners studying abroad. Even in a highly open society such as the US, total immersion is not feasible for some. A learner may not be able to find an American host family. Immigration laws may forbid her to work in a US business. Her inadequate English language ability may not allow her to enroll in a regular academic program. For American learners abroad, they are likely to encounter more challenges, particularly in those less-open societies. For instance, until recently, the Chinese government's regulations make it almost impossible for a learner to stay with a Chinese host family. Consequently, many study abroad programs have to house their learners in "international learner dorms," separated from Chinese learners. Sometimes, a seemingly trivial issue poses a challenge. For some American learners, the difference in academic calendars between the home and the foreign institutions prevents them from enrolling in an academic program at a foreign university. Academic programs in most countries, including the US, are not willing to take a learner in for less than a semester. The most obvious challenge for immersing into the local academic and professional culture is the learner's ability to use the target language. Similar to the ESL situation in the US, lower-level learners are not linguistically prepared to take regular courses taught in the target language. Consequently, they are placed into a "sheltered" language class – sheltered from native speakers of the language. It is fair to say that study abroad programs are scattered along a continuum from "an island in a foreign sea" to "total immersion."

To design a study abroad curriculum for Superior-level learners, we should first consider their special needs. Superior-level learners have mastered the general skills and knowledge of the target language and have progressed to the stage of applying the language to professional use. In other words, they are at the stage of creating with the language, such as interacting with professionals in the host country, writing a research paper, making a professional presentation for a formal gathering, etc. The creative process is highly individualized. Accordingly, the curriculum design also needs to be individualized.

Depth of processing research indicates that the presentation of coherent and meaningful information brings about deeper processing, which results in better learning. Cummins (1992) proposes a distinction between two levels of language proficiency: surface-level basic interpersonal communicative skills (BICS), which involves cognitive processes of learning knowledge, comprehension, and application, and the deeper level of cognitive/academic language proficiency (CALP), which requires such cognitive processes as analysis, synthesis, and evaluation. As CALP requires more complex language abilities, it is best taught within a framework that manipulates more complex and authentic content. For near-native learners, content-based language instruction is a common practice. Our curriculum should facilitate Superior-level learners to access the disciplinary courses at local universities. Depending on the learner's academic or professional field, she should be able to enroll directly in the local university's chemistry or political science program, studying the subject matters of her choice, interacting with peers in her field, and immersing into the local academic or professional culture.

In addition to content learning, we may consider using an adjunct model for language training. The adjunct model originally refers to learners being enrolled concurrently in two linked courses, a content course and a language course. In our case, it can be a customized "directed study" arrangement.

Language training is tied into the learner's course work or research at the local university and the socio-pragmatic contexts of the host culture. Such a course is learner centered. The learner lets the teachers know what she needs. They design a learning plan that considers the learner's current proficiency level (including strengths and weaknesses in all language and culture areas), learning styles, professional interests and needs, and opportunities for learning. The teacher's major role is to encourage independent learning, by directing the learner to useful language resources and effective strategies to solve a problem. In summary, the curriculum should effectively prepare learners for the course requirements, cultural differences, and teaching styles of the host university, enhance their engagement in the intellectual, political, cultural, and social institutions of the host country, and encourage independent learning.

Apart from formal academic learning, we should take advantage of the native speech community. An effective method is to integrate academic learning with out-of-classroom activities. Asking learners to accomplish some meaningful learning tasks pushes them to interact with the local residents. Content-related field trips, interviews with local businesses and residents, gathering research data, giving speeches to local communities are some examples of such learning tasks. Formal classroom study is not the only—or even the primary—educational goal of some learners who study abroad. Equally or more attractive to many are the possibilities afforded by overseas study for internships, apprenticeships, and fieldwork. Such opportunities broaden the learner's experience in preparation for careers in business, law, education, the foreign service, social work, etc. Study abroad programs that offer and support "experiential learning" are growing. "Experiential education" sets study abroad apart from learning at a traditional discipline-based institution (Lutterman-Aguilar and Gingerichl, 2002). Experiential education means that education is rooted in and transformed by experience.

Learning takes place as people test concepts and theories in their experience and as they develop new concepts and theories based upon their experiences. Working for a local organization is beneficial to language learning as learners are exposed to interactions at the workplace. By participating in problem solving and dealing with special terminology and discourse in a professional field, learners use, reflect, and fine tune their linguistic, sociolinguistic, and content knowledge. Learning through working induces the gains of advanced language competence, which is symbolized by the ability to understand the meaning of linguistic variation in a range of different socio-pragmatic contexts. An alternative of internship is for learners to volunteer in local communities. Work or service in the native speech community puts language to use and gives life to knowledge acquired in classrooms.

A major component of study abroad is living in the native speech community. Home stays have been attractive to many, as opposed to dormitory living at an academic institution. By living with a local family, learners are exposed not only to the target language, but also to the target culture. Many details in local life, such as special cooking ingredients and techniques, child-rearing practice, interaction among families and relatives, etc., are hard to grasp, if the learner has not lived with the locals. It is these small details that separate a learner from the Superior level to the Distinguished. Without correct cultural references, it is impossible to sound like a near-native speaker. One concern with host families is whether they are typical families in the host country. Generally speaking, families willing to host a foreign learner are often more internationally minded and more affluent. We should try to recruit families from various social and economic strata. Other advantageous living arrangements include pairing a local learner with an American learner in a dorm setting or encouraging learners to live independently in a local community. Such living arrangements force learners to interact more with the native speakers.

The final aspect is on learner training. The extent to which the language (be it oral or written) is learned depends on numerous variables, including individual differences in learners' learning styles, motivation, and aptitude. Although Superior-level learners score higher on motivation and aptitude than most learners, it is always a good idea to make them aware of different learning strategies that may help them in various situations.

In summary, study abroad is different from study at a home institution. The major difference lies in the language environment. We should intentionally utilize the language environment and the international experience as the basis for learning and incorporate formal language training with learners' living and working experience abroad.

Being in country is not enough for learners to make progress in proficiency. Learners need to be well prepared linguistically. They need to have a structured program of study as well as opportunities to interact with native speakers. They need to be in country for a fairly long period of time. Having examined the experiences of over 3200 learners, a longitudinal study of learners of Russian abroad found several factors which predict proficiency gains in immersion settings: notably, that longer-term programs give exponentially better results than short-term ones.

- After three months, 55% of learners starting with an S/2 showed no measurable gain in proficiency. 38% moved to a 2+ and 7% moved to a 3.
- After ten months, 38% showed no gain, 31% moved to a 2+ and 31% improved to a 3.
- Learners studying in Russia for the summer did not improve their speaking or reading scores.
- Grammar is important. Learners who knew their grammar going into the program did well.

- Good pre-departure skills in speaking, reading, and listening indicate success on an immersion, with listening being the least important.
- Age matters. Younger learners seemed to do better than older ones (age range was 18-32 with a mean age of 22). Learners who started studying Russian in High School did better than those who started in college.
- Gender is not a factor in success.

This longitudinal study was conducted by ACTR for more than 25 years. The kinds of data that have been collected are unique for their richness in the world language field and are a goldmine for researchers into what works and does not work in study abroad programs.

Further Reading

Cummins, Jim. 1992. Language proficiency, bilingualism, and academic achievement. In *The Multicultural Classroom: Readings for Content- Area Teachers* (Richard-Amato & Snow). Reading, Mass.: Addison-Wesley.

Davidson, Dan E., Garas, N, & Lekić, Maria D. 2021. "Transformative Language Learning in the Overseas Language Environment: Exploring Affordances of Intercultural Development." In *Transformative Language Learning and Teaching* (Leaver, Davidson, & Campbell). Cambridge, UK: Cambridge University Press.

Lutterman-Aguilar, Ann & Oval Gingerichl. 2002. Experiential Pedagogy for Study Abroad: Educating for Global Citizenship. *Frontiers: The Interdisciplinary Journal of Study Abroad: Volume VIII*: 41-82

13

Incorporate Games, Music, Folklore, and School Subjects

Michael Morrisey
(University of Kassel, Germany)

Many of the same activities can be used at Level 4 that are used at lower levels, but the orientation is significantly different. Folk songs, for example, are usually associated with the elementary stages of language learning and young learners, but they can also be a rich source of cultural, historical, and linguistic enrichment for adults.

Only a minority of folk songs are children's songs. Most have serious themes which preserve not so much the facts of history as the voices of the people who lived it. In the words of Mary Robinson, the president of Ireland, referring to the Great Famine of 1845-50:

We celebrate those people in our past not for their power, not for their victory...but for the profound dignity of human survival. We honor our people by taking our folk memory of this catastrophe into the present world with us and allowing it to strengthen and deepen our identity with those who are still suffering [opening the famine museum at Strokestown House, Co. Roscommon, 1994].

In one of the most famous, and often heard, songs of the Famine, "Skibbereen," a father tells his son of their eviction from their land because he could not pay the rent, of the death of his wife after the eviction, and of his subsequent involvement in revolutionary activities. Like many songs written by exiles in America, this one ends with the hope of someday returning with an army of Fenians to free the homeland

Oh, father dear, I often hear you speak of Erin's isle
Her lofty scenes, her valleys green, her mountains rude and wild
They say it is a lovely land, wherein a prince might dwell
Then why did you abandon it, the reason to me tell
My son, I loved my native land with energy and pride
Till a blight came o'er my crops, my sheep and cattle died
The rent and taxes were to pay, and I could not them redeem
And that's the cruel reason that I left old Skibbereen
Oh, well I do remember that bleak November day
When the bailiff and the landlord came to drive us all away
They set the roof on fire with their cursed English spleen
And that's another reason I left old Skibbereen
Your mother, too, God rest her soul, lay on the snowy ground
She fainted in her anguish seeing the desolation round
She never rose but passed away, from life to immortal dreams
And that's another reason, I left old Skibbereen
And well do I remember the year of forty-eight
When I arose with Erin's sons to fight against the state
I was hunted through the mountains as a traitor to the Queen
And that's another reason why I left old Skibbereen
And you were only two years old, and feeble was your frame
I could not leave you with my friends, for you bore your father's name
I wrapped you in my cotamore [heavy overcoat] in the dead of night unseen
And I heaved a sigh and bade goodbye to dear old Skibbereen
Oh, father dear, the day may come when on vengeance we will call
And Irishmen both stout and tall will rally unto the call

I'll be the man to lead the van beneath the flag of green
And loud and high we'll raise the cry, Revenge for Skibbereen

Almost every line of the song offers opportunities to discuss and expatiate upon the historical and cultural context, as well as the linguistic features of the text itself. Distinguished-level learners are able, and should be encouraged, to do this research themselves, by using resources such as the *Oxford English Dictionary*.

In a lighter vein, songs can challenge not only the learner's historical and cultural understanding but also his articulatory apparatus. In one version of "The Bold O'Donoghue," the singer(s) is called upon to imitate, in jocular fashion, various contemporary English accents:

Well, here I am from Paddy's land, a land of high renown
I broke the hearts of all the girls for miles round Keady town
And when they hear that I'm away they'll raise a hullabaloo
When they hear about that handsome lad they call O'Donoghue
[Ch] For I'm the boy to please her, and I'm the boy to squeeze her
I'm the boy to tease her, and I'll tell you what I'll do
I'll court her like an Irishman, wi' me brogue and blarney too is me plan
With the holligan, swolligan, rolligan, molligan bold O'Donoghue
Well I hear that Queen Victoria has a daughter fine and grand
Perhaps she'd take it into her head for to marry an Irishman
And if I could only get the chance to speak a word or two
I know she'd take a notion to the bold O'Donoghue
I wish me love was a red red rose growing on yonder wall
And me to be a dewdrop and upon her brow I'd fall
Perhaps now she might think of me as a rather heavy dew
No more she'd love the handsome lad they call O'Donoghue
[Englishman] Well, here I am from England, a land of high renown

I've broken the hearts of all the girls for miles from London town

And when they hear that I'm away they'll raise a dickens, hurrah

When they hear about that handsome fellow they called O'Donogha

[Ch] For I'm the fellow to please ha, and I'm the fellow to squeeze ha

I'm the chap to tease ha, and I'll tell you what I shall do

I shall court her like an Englishman, with a brogue and blarney too is my plan

With the holligan, swolligan, rolligan, molligan bold O'Donogha

[Indian] Well, here I am from India, a land of high renown

I have broken the hearts of lots of girls for miles from Delhi town

And when they see that I am away they will raise one awful row

When they hear about that handsome fellow they call Sahib O'Donoghow

[Ch] For I am the fellow to please her you see, I am the fellow to squeeze her you see

I am the boy to tease her, I will tell you what I will do

I will court her like an Indian man, with my turban tied as well as I can

With the holligan, swolligan, rolligan, molligan Sahib O'Donoghue

To these can be added verses by an "American," a "German," a "Frenchman," a "Chinese," etc. The psychological benefits of self-deprecatory humor should not be overlooked; for once the learner cannot reveal his imperfections, even exaggerate them, and receive appreciation rather than correction! The same can be said of joke-telling.

Language play—with puns, jokes, and accents—is an important factor in near-native proficiency. The Level-4 learner should be able to understand, appreciate, and participate in humor in the L2 much the same as a native speaker does. This ability requires a dialectal and stylistic range and flexibility that cannot be expected at lower levels.

Singing can also bring out this flexibility and depth. Although professional singers can sometimes imitate native-like pronunciation in a world language, this takes a lot of practice and is generally limited to a particular song. It is not a skill they can apply spontaneously. A Level-4 speaker, however—provided s/he has a taste for singing—can often hear, reproduce, and create the same kind of subtle and spontaneous modulations of voice that come naturally to native speakers, both in singing and in normal speech. Singing is thus an appropriate but different kind of challenge for learners at Level 4 than at lower levels of proficiency.

Further Reading

Morrissey, Michael D. 2001. *Song and Story: An Anthology of Irish Folk Songs.* Norderstedt, Germany: Books on Demand.

Harte, Frank and Donal Lunny. 2004. *The Hungry Voice: The Song Legacy of Ireland's Great Hunger.* Dublin: Hummingbird Records.

14

Tapping into Learner Motivation with Authentic Texts

Olla Al-Shalchi
(University of Texas at Austin)

Using authentic material in the language classroom is essential. It not only helps build learners vocabulary and grammar but gives them an insight into the culture of the region. During the early stages in learning a language, it may be challenging to find appropriate authentic materials, but when learners are at the Advanced level aiming toward Superior-level proficiency, that challenge no longer exists and the sky is the limit with the authentic texts available. Additionally, authentic material motivates learners to continue learning the language because they see that they are closer than ever to reaching professional proficiency. Learners feel accomplished and proud when they are able to work with texts that were intended for native speakers.

At the Advanced level, learners after have mastered the most common grammatical structures and have learned thousands vocabulary items, and it is important to have them continue to be pushed to add on their vocabulary and expand their knowledge of the region as much as possible. It is with language that we are able to comprehend and learn and spark a fire and dig deeper in an area of interest. For this reason, the topics that learners study need to be areas of interest, current and relevant, and allow for debate and discussion in which there is no easy solution.

In my own Arabic class, learners are exposed to topics that they may not have thought about and/or may have limited background information on. For example, I teach a fourth-year Arabic class in which learners are presented with units about various societal issues that affect communities throughout the world. Learners learn about women's rights, artificial intelligence, living through a pandemic, and poverty and hunger. All of these units are studied from various points of view: historical, economical, religious, and literary, for example.

To give a clearer understanding of how authentic texts are used, I present to you more detail about the unit that deals with poverty and hunger, and the many different angles that are studied within this unit. Learners learn about the role of different religions in terms of poverty and hunger and what these religions say about helping those in need. Televised interviews with scholars and religious figures are viewed. From an economical perspective, learners examine which countries and ethnicities have the greatest percentages of people living below the poverty line and factors that contribute to poverty and how to prevent it in the future. From a literature perspective, learners read Ghassan Kanafani's short, powerful novel, *Men in the Sun*, which tells the story of different men who are so desperate to go after a better life to get away from living in poverty that they are smuggled in an empty water tank in the scorching summer day across a desert. None of the men survive the journey, and although the story is non-fiction, it is a clear representation of the despair and struggle that so many people went through during the 1950s-1960s and continue to go through. Learners also study in depth at the aftermath of the Iraqi society dealing with U.N. sanctions which lead the country to have tone of the worst healthcare systems, suffering of malnutrition, an increase in death rates, and a lack in education. A native doctor of the country was invited as a guest speaker in class, and learners were able to hear firsthand how it was to live under these conditions. Not only were they learning about a region they did not know much about, they were learning about how an entire society did/did not survive such strict sanctions.

In this one unit, not only are learners exposed to the topics of hunger and poverty, but they do so in a way that gives them a representation of a variety of facts from different points of view all within the same topic. This practice provides learners with a thirst to continue learning about the topic, all while being committed to using authentic texts in the world language. Learners are motivated to continue study of the language because they find these topics and materials—entirely in the target language—interesting and compelling.

Further Reading

Arechiga, Debbie. 2012. *Reaching English Language Learners in Every Classroom: Energizers for Teaching and Learning.* New York: Routledge. https://doi.org/10.4324/9781315856186

Kanafānī, Ghassān. 1991. *Men in the Sun and Other Palestinian stories.* Cairo: American University in Cairo Press.

15

The Importance of Models, The Power of Imitation!

Cynthia Martin
(University of Maryland, College Park)

We give lots of models to language learners at the lower levels, asking them to memorize and imitate those models over and over until they start to be able to manipulate parts of them and then create new variations of them on their own spontaneously, relying first on chunks of that memorized language, gradually moving to genuine personalized creation. In other words, we have them *pretend* to be the next level of proficiency long before they actually can sustain that level spontaneously (this is *performance* toward proficiency). Inexplicably, we often abandon this approach as we work with learners at Intermediate and Advanced. If we want learners to move from Intermediate to Advanced, or Advanced to Superior, or even beyond, then they need to have good models of what that looks and sounds like. If learners are already at the Advanced level of proficiency, they have a fairly large generic vocabulary and good structural control over high-frequency structures, partial control over lower frequency structures, and the ability to organize their discourse into what we think of as oral paragraphs. Growing their lexical breath and improving their structural control is not enough to move into the Superior range, where they need to be able to discuss ideas and issues, support various opinions and positions, and hypothesize about potential implications of certain actions or inactions. One effective, I would say essential strategy, is to provide learners with models of authentic interactions, examples of real conversations of speakers at this level discussing issues and ideas. The objective is to have learners imitate, rehearse (dare I say *memorize*) passages from these interactions and *perform* them as though they were their own. We can find these models in authentic television and radio programs of the "talking heads" sort, widely available today in most languages on the Internet. First identify a few such sources that present interesting and engaging issues, and then either choose specific programs for learners to watch or listen to, or have learners chose from the program's site based on personal interest. I like to use sources that have subtitles (closed captions) in the target language as an additional input. Direct learners to pay attention not just to *what* is being discussed, i.e., content, but also to the *linguistic formulations* being used at this level. For example, after listening once or twice to understand the basic content, you might ask them to pull out and list all the ways a speaker introduces an argument or respectfully disagrees with someone and then presents an alternative view. Learners then watch and re-watch or listen and re-listen with the aim of essentially memorizing and imitating what they hear from one (or more) of the participants in the discussion. The ultimate aim is to treat these passages like scripts that learners then perform, like actors (another reason I prefer programs that provide written transcripts). If learners are already firmly in the Advanced range, say AM or AH, they can clearly memorize a page or two of text. Repeat this strategy with diverse content, looking for patterns in linguistic structures, discourse organization, lexical precision, etc. Learners can take a passage and manipulate it slightly, focusing on one or two features, for example, try to render a similar passage by changing the subject or timeframe, or by swapping in different verbal or adjectival synonyms that might work in the given context, etc. Over time, learners begin to internalize these features, ultimately weaving them together spontaneously on their own in non-scripted, non-scaffolded contexts, helping them to cross over into the Superior range.

As the Russian expression reminds us: *Repetition is the mother of learning!* No matter the targeted proficiency level, there is simply no substitute for time-on-task repeating and practicing what one wants to be able to do spontaneously long before one can actually do so.

[This modest contribution was inspired by Boris Shekhtman, a legendary figure in the field, who helped countless learners of Russian, including many working for the US government and journalists, to achieve very high levels of proficiency in Russian. Though I did not have the opportunity to study with Boris, I did have the pleasure of meeting him on a few occasions. Among his many contributions, he was a proponent of using models and memorization at all levels, and I have benefitted enormously, as have my students, from his work.]

Further Reading

Chamot, Anna Uhl. 2004. "Issues in Language Learning Strategy Research and Teaching." *Electronic Journal of Foreign Language Teaching* 1(1): 14-26.

Thomas Jesús Garza, Ed. D.

16

Oral Plagiarism: Transcription and Chunking to Get to Distinguished

Richard Robin
(The George Washington University)

The Superior's lament. One of my former students, upon passing the Superior borderline told me ruefully, "Now I can say whatever I want, but not exactly the way I want. When does *that* happen?"

It happens at Distinguished, of course. But getting there requires lots of components. One of the most prominent among them is a dramatic increase in control over vocabulary and word worder — a final farewell to subject/agent domination of the left side of the sentence. To that end Sibrina (2008) came up with lists of less frequent, register-appropriate words and collocations. Learners using such lists would then try and work the new vocabulary into usable contexts. Such an approach continues a common practice used at lower levels: introducing vocabulary to be activated. But at the Superior level, learners have more organic options to increasing repertoire: oral plagiarism made possible by transcription and chunking.

Force-fed noticing. Effective language learners are good noticers. They quickly identify phenomena in the target language (mostly vocabulary, but also other features) that fill linguistic holes. That process starts much earlier as learners in country at the Advanced level begin to replace sentences constructed through a mix of recombination and translation with native-sounding repertoire. **Почему это плохо** becomes **чем это плохо**. **Это плохо** is replaced by **Кому это нужно**. But unstructured noticing in largely top-down activities (read: making sense of what you hear) takes learners only so far. Even structured instruction provides a garden-hose stream of language, not the fire hose required for the leap from Superior to Distinguished.

The fire hydrant comes in the form of recorded talk sites, such as Russian talk radio *Ekho Moskvy*, YouTube opinion pieces, or podcasts at a high level of discourse. Unfortunately, even good noticers are likely to discard much of what they hear as they concentrate on the content of what is said rather than the language. We can relieve the cognitive distraction of comprehension (!) with a bottom-up activity: transcription.

Transcription is force-fed noticing in two or even three modalities — listening, writing and, in some cases, speaking, as described further down. It involves short-term memory processing of sophisticated language. And it is largely autonomous.

Autonomous learners can speed up the transcription process with text-to-speech (TTS) technology. They play a few sentences of the original recording to themselves and dictate what they hear into a Google document. They can and should use Google's Russian spellchecker as an initial guide to accuracy. But they must avoid the temptation to have Google do the transcription for them. (Another temptation is to peek prematurely at the site's transcript of the talk — if there is one.)

Leveraging autonomy. The existence of the Language Flagship programs is testimony to the efforts over the last few decades to provide explicit instruction that leads learners from Superior to Distinguished. But at the Flagship level autonomous learning becomes the principal vehicle for further language acquisition. Nevertheless, in group settings, still common at high levels of instruction, program directors and instructors make assumptions about the lexical lacunae of the participants. They then seek to *push* that vocabulary into the learners' already existing language framework. Transcription is concentrated autonomous learning. Instructors don't push; learners *pull* language out of high-level discourse of their own choosing based on self-perceived needs. The self-didactive nature of transcription should stimulate internalization and use of transcribed phrases.

Of course, "should stimulate" and is far from "does stimulate"—a proposition that takes no small amount of formal investigation. So, transcription, for the time being, is to be considered an experimental pedagogy. But the anecdotal evidence from a handful of learners who have crossed over the Superior line (or are quite close) provides grounds to continue such an experiment. Learners talk about finding language that fills rhetorical holes that they themselves feel, even if their interlocutors insist that they hear no serious lexical lacunae. That makes sense. Superiors are experts at covering hiding their weaknesses. But that doesn't mean that they do not feel those weaknesses.

A few examples. A sample of expressions that I have heard learners take from transcription to spontaneous speech include structural devices such as freeing the subject-agent from its leftmost position, e.g., **Меня мало беспокоят такие фразеологизмы** and rhetorical questions as paragraph openers accompanied by answers, e.g., **А почему так надо? А так надо.** Individual vocabulary items are often rhetorically richer replacements for common words, such as **порой**, **сложившийся, составляющая, нынешний, крохотный, чуждый,**

Procedures. Experimenting with learner transcription of high-level texts raises a number of questions that probably don't have definitive answers without empirical data. But for now, we can make some educated guesses

Should transcribers work on Superior-level or on Distinguished-level talk? Paradoxically, I would suggest sticking to speech at the Superior or Superior High level, even if our goal is to create a stairway to Distinguished. Let's remember that the high-register texts we label Distinguished for the *receptive* skills are almost never examples of spontaneous speech. We don't expect Distinguished speakers to give us *zaum*. We expect them to handle Superior topics, but with greater expressive breadth, unmarred by stylistic or lexical deficiencies. (I am not addressing the lower-register end of the Distinguished speech-range, although we could ask leaners to transcribe children's science shows.)

Should transcribers have access to the original transcript? Many sites provide both an audio and written record. YouTube tries to caption everything with speech recognition. But checking against an official transcript is probably not necessary or desirable, as long as transcription gaps are not that frequent. After all, the goal is to have learners target rhetorical devices that are likely to stick, not those that are far beyond the learner's periphery of comfort. Nevertheless, such decisions are best left to autonomous learners, who have already demonstrated the linguistic wherewithal to reach Superior.

Make yourself useful. In a perfect world, Superior-level speakers are, on the one hand, motivated to spend concentrated amounts of time making private transcripts for the purposes of language gain. I wouldn't count on that enthusiasm lasting too long. On the other hand, the world needs transcripts and captions. Learners who can fill in any gaps in their transcriptions of YouTube videos can offer them to the channel-owners directly or donate them to subtitles. org, where they become available to YouTube viewers who have installed the Agora browser plug-in. That way learning can be productive for the learner and for the rest of us.

Further Reading

Sibrina, Svetlana. 2008. *Обучение фразеологическим единицам студентов-иностранцев высокого продвинутого уровня in Shekhtman, Boris (ed.) Методическая разработка по преподаванию социокультурной компетенции студентам высокого продвинутого уровня (на материале русского языка).*

Thomas Jesús Garza, Ed. D.

17

Theater As a Bridge to
Superior-Level Proficiency

Antonella Del Fatorre-Olson
(University of Texas at Austin)

Performing arts are a powerful tool in teaching and learning language and culture and bring learners to the Superior level of proficiency in the target language. Bringing together literary and cultural components with a linguistic interaction gives the opportunity of full immersion: learners do not just study and analyze a play; rather they *are* the characters. As Stanislavski writes in *An Actor Prepares*, "characters cannot be 'shown,' they can only be lived," thus learners are encouraged to think and behave as the characters in the specific historical and cultural period in which the play is set. The knowledge of history and culture becomes, therefore, a relevant part in the learning process as well as building a community.

Cultural globalization goes together with the notion of "Transculturalism," that is "seeing oneself in the other." Teaching a foreign language through theater provides a good foundation for reaching a global and transcultural knowledge. The theatrical component plays an important role in giving learners the chance to deal with thought-provoking material while satisfying the need to enhance their language competence. Therefore, a class that focuses primarily on the analysis, adaptation and *mise-en-scène* of theatrical works ending with public performances of a full-fledged play at the end of the semester is a worthwhile method to bring learners to the Superior level. Such a course also creates a strong community among students since in order for it to be successful, respect, openness, inclusion, acceptance of diversity, and freedom of expression are crucial elements. Through performing art skills, the goals that can be reached are a deeper understanding of the culture and history, progress in the target language and improvement in the pronunciation and intonation. The latter is particularly important; in fact, while pronunciation is stressed at all levels of instruction, the same cannot be said for intonation, which is crucial to obtaining Superior-level proficiency and is easily achievable when learners focus on acting and performing.

A pedagogical approach in teaching this class can be inspired by some of Stanislavski's notions:

- "The external plane" and "the plane of social situations" are applied when the historical background and the plot of the play are discussed.
- "The literary plane" consists in the analysis of the ideas and style of the play.
- Emotional memory (relating to own personal experiences) is an aid in the memorization of lines and interpretation of the character.

While the first weeks of the semester are devoted to analyzing the play and its author ("the external and literary planes"), during the rest of the semester a transformation takes place: the class becomes a theatrical company with learners as actors/co-directors/stage managers/ costume and set designers and the instructor their director. Memorization of lines (through emotional memory) and intonation constitute valid instruments to focus on the importance of each single word and on the proper way it should be delivered. Moreover, adding gestures and facial expressions to the performance opens the door to discussing everyday culture.

Although I have been offering classical modern theatrical pieces over the course of the years, in my Italian Drama Workshop upper division class, recently I am finding that narrative theater (*teatro di narrazione*) is a genre of particular interest: in fact, it is a unique theatrical form in which the narrator-actor keeps the oral tradition alive by narrating history, micro or macro, from a personal point of view. In the narrative theater all plays are monologues and, if there are multiple characters in the play, the "narr-actor" interprets all of them; therefore, there is ample space for an interactive collaboration among the learners and the teacher: together they will transform the monologues into dialogues. Indeed, it is a challenging task, but one that can harmonize the understanding of a complex historical context with the application of language acquisition.

In order to make the learners the real participants in the process of learning and solidifying their community as storytellers, they must create something tangible to share with everyone such as a website. While learners study the play and its author, analyzing their character and memorizing lines, they design a website, which helps them clarify the meaning of the play and its social and historical background. Moreover, learners should be responsible for creating the advertisement material including the brochure (written program of the show) and a short video to be used as a trailer. For each member of the class, the focus is no longer on a textbook but on building a community; therefore, the success of the final performance is in the hands of the community that has been created. The grade is not the end-goal but rather the by-product of a semester-long experience of learning and growing together in the target language. For the learners, very few of whom are professional actors, standing on stage and hearing the applause after the final curtain is the mark of a semester well earned.

Further Reading

Maley, Alan, & Duff, Alan. 2005. *Drama Techniques: A Resource Book of Communication Activities for Language Teachers, 3rd ed.* Cambridge: Cambridge University Press.

Winston, Joe. 2011. *Second Language Learning through Drama: Practical Techniques and Applications.* New York: Routledge.

18

Simulations in Upper-Level Courses

Irina Walsh
(Bryn Mawr College)

In target language (TL) content-based courses, instructors typically choose presentations and papers as the final assessment of learners' progress. Other instructors, however, give up these traditional assessment instruments in favor of final projects, which engage learners in more contextualized, real-life, higher-stakes tasks. One type of projects are simulations, which provide an opportunity for authentic, meaningful, and memorable experiences in the TL. For a final project in a literature course taught in the TL, learners can participate in a simulated academic conference, following all of its typical stages.

In order to participate in a real academic conference, each person writes a proposal, receives peer-reviewed feedback on it, and after the paper is accepted, each participant registers for the conference and writes a paper. Then, each conference participant delivers a presentation in a panel or a roundtable and answers questions from the audience. A course participant will go through all of these stages, from submitting a proposal to writing the actual paper, as part of the simulation. Depending on the course type, simulations can also include buying airplane tickets and making reservations at the conference hotel, mingling in an informal conference reception, or submitting a paper for a conference proceedings publication.

Because of their multi-stage nature, these simulations take time to design and develop and may require input not only from the instructor but also from the Library Information and Technology Services, Language labs, and other campus resources. To build a highly contextualized academic conference simulation, an instructor needs a simulated "conference website," "a conference administrator" and "proposal reviewers," a keynote speaker, a discussant, and an audience for the conference session. The more of these components are present in the simulation, the more authentic it will be. Since the roles of the "conference administrator" and the "proposal reviewers" do not require any public appearance, they can be played by the instructor of the course. The simulation will feel more authentic, however, if a real keynote speaker, discussant, and a conference audience participate in it.

Such a project can serve not only as a cumulative assessment but also as a language learning opportunity for learners. Indeed, in order to submit a proposal, learners need to know how to write a compelling proposal. Likewise, to deliver a presentation during a conference, participants should know how to structure a presentation and how to deliver it effectively in a way appropriate in the target culture, including norms of genre and register.

The learning component of the academic conference simulation will then consist of a number of tasks that help learners a) write a conference proposal and b) prepare a presentation. The course instructor will need to develop or use existing materials for this component of the simulation. Learners can engage with the learning materials in class or using blended-learning tools outside of the classroom. In the latter case, the instructor will need to decide which technological tools to use in these blended learning materials (H5P, Flipgrid, Extempore make helpful products).

Learners benefit from well-structured projects in various ways. From the linguistic standpoint, such a simulation enhances learners' formal oral and written presentational skills. Furthermore, by using the language in an authentic way, navigating a multi-stage, complex, real-life project, and engaging with a community of practice, learners deliver a higher quality product that serves as a meaningful form of assessment, but also a learning opportunity at the end of a course.

Further Reading

Gras-Velázquez, Adrián. 2020. *Project-Based Learning in Second Language Acquisition: Building Communities of Practice in Higher Education.* New York: Routledge.

Section III

Focus on the Instructor

19

Break Limiting Forms of
Strategic Competence

Betty Lou Leaver
(Defense Language Institute Foreign Language Center)

The development of strategic competence has been a focus of teachers of learners at lower levels of proficiency for some time. Teachers using communicative approaches in particular have strongly advocated the teaching of strategies that allow learners to cope with authentic materials (materials written or spoken by native speakers and intended to be read or heard by other native speakers) at very low levels of proficiency when their linguistic skills are not adequately developed for complete understanding or expression. "Adapt the task and not the text" is the adage, an important one for both content-based instruction and task-based instruction as well as the more generic communicative methods; underlying this adage is the concept that in order to complete the task learners will have to use compensation strategies (e.g., guessing from context, applying background knowledge, and circumlocution). As learners develop in proficiency, their use of compensation strategies gets stronger and stronger, to the point that these strategies allow them to participate in nearly any social event or accomplish nearly any informal task assigned to them. They can even use compensation strategies to handle many professional work requirements. The definition of Superior-Level proficiency incorporates an ability to use compensation strategies in quite sophisticated ways and liberal doses.

Unfortunately, the definition of Distinguished-Level proficiency does *not* accommodate the use of compensation strategies. Instead of needing to paraphrase when encountering new lexical demands, learners are expected to possess a deep and broad vocabulary that is not only adequate to the task of description and connotation but is highly refined and able to project denotations and implications. Likewise, their lexical and structural knowledge must be broad enough to decode not only what is stated but also what is implied and sort it by register, dialect, and deviation, if any, from standard speech. Well-developed compensation strategies and an inculcated habit of using them get in the way of reaching this higher level of refinement. For this reason, teachers must force learners to leave their compensation strategies behind, to leave the comfortable plateau of using what they know and what is at hand, and to practice using what native speakers use. It is no longer appropriate to "come close." They must hit the target in all areas of lexical precision, structural accuracy, and appropriate register.

At the same time, metacognitive strategy development, which is often forgotten at lower levels or not as possible with the same level of understanding of the learning process and with the same amount of self-awareness as at higher levels, can be critically important. Asking learners to reflect on their language use, learning experiences, and linguistic success and failure in work and social settings can do much to develop the metacognitive strategies that they will need for the remainder of their careers as professional language users.

Further Reading

Leaver, Betty Lou. 2002. *Achieving Native-Like Second-Language Proficiency: A Catalogue of Critical Factors: Volume 1: Speaking.* Salinas, CA: MSI Press.

Leaver, Betty Lou. 2003. "Nine Errors in SLA Philosophy." *ACTR Letter 30* (1): 1-7.

Leaver, Betty Lou, & Shekhtman, Boris. 2002. "Principles and Practices in Teaching Superior-Level Language Skills: Not Just More of the Same." In *Developing Professional-Level Language Proficiency*, Betty Lou Leaver & Boris Shekhtman, eds. Cambridge: Cambridge University Press.

20

Close the Gap between Native Speaker/ Non-Native Speaker Communicative Differences

Surendra Gambhir
(University of Pennsylvania)

In order for learners to reach native-like levels, it is essential that they understand the communicative differences of native speakers and non-native speakers, in other words, the reality within which they live and communicate. Good high-level programs take into account the nature of these differences and help the learner striving for native-like proficiency to learn how to use an understanding of the nuances of native speaker-nonnative speaker communication to close the gap between his or her language skills and those of the native speaker with whom he or she is communicating.

High-level learners specifically need to understand the difference between the content of speech (meaning) and the form of the utterance/writing (language). When native speakers talk there is generally a complete coincidence of meaning and language, and the listener is not aware of any struggle that the speaker is having with linguistic forms and word choices, i.e., with the mechanics of the language. Rather, the ideas dominate.

One of the goals of the classroom instruction at high levels of proficiency, then, is to help the learner move to this same kind of communication where ideas dominate and mechanics are as automatic as they are in the native speaker's communication, where the concentration is on *what* he or she is saying without a need to pay attention to *how* he or she is saying it. Whereas at lower levels of proficiency, it is acceptable and normal for learners to separate the ideational and mechanical planes of communication, at the Distinguished level they need to approach as closely as possible the amount of coincidence that is found in native-speaker communication.

The successful teacher of highly proficient learners begins by showing learners the most important attributes of native speakers' performance: fluency, readiness, high level of communication control, and ability to use complex structures. For that purpose, teachers of Superior-Distinguished learners develop special exercises that correspond to specific communicative goals. For example, at the SLTC, four kinds of exercises are used to bring a Superior-level learner closer to the native speaker's performance:

1. Conversation Maintenance Exercises.

2. Preparatory Exercises.

3. Conversation Controlling Exercises

4. Complication Exercises.

Conversation Maintenance Exercises teach learners to speak fast, readily, spontaneous and without efforts. Successful teachers help learners gain the ability to maintain verbal contact by requiring them to practice giving as long and detailed answers as possible to any question of a native speaker; these exercises teach learners to "hold the floor," to produce an unlimited amount of speech, and to control deliberately the amount of talking they do. These exercises also train learners to use only automatically controlled patterns. Even native speakers generally choose to be close to their "comfort zones" (i.e., their automatically controlled patterns) when speaking. For non-native speakers, such control is even more important.

Preparatory Exercises help learners to accumulate a wide range of vocabulary by developing their ability to talk on various and specific topics. As their name implies, preparatory exercises prepare learners for what is ahead: for questions connected with these topics—so that they are ready when native speakers ask questions that are difficult for them.

Conversation Controlling Exercises train learners to have complete command of grammar and language interrogative system, various management expressions, and highly effective comprehension technique. Teachers in Superior-Distinguished programs help learners to develop the ability and predilection for using a wide range of question types, reflecting the great variety of question forms available within a given language, including sophisticated syntactic constructions. (Culturally appropriate and linguistically varied question discourse, for some reason, is often ignored in lower-level classrooms.) These exercises also teach learners how to survive in the language environment when they have to communicate not with one, but with many native speakers, and they help learners to understand the specific intricate details of what being said by a native speaker.

Complication Exercises provide learners with the opportunity to practice embellishing their speech in literate ways. In this way, these exercises help learners to acquire sophisticated grammatical expressions, infrequent linguistic elements, intricate discourse elements, socio-linguistically appropriate expressions, nonstandard dialects, slang, and greater lexical precision. They require learners to replace less sophisticated, fossilized forms of speech with more appropriate, more refined, more sophisticated expressions, e.g., the use of metaphors, similes, hyperbole, synecdoche, personification, onomatopoeia, and the like. Complication exercises especially well prepare learners for the most serious kinds of communication: problem-solving discussion, interpreting language and culture, interview, briefing, presentation, debate, negotiation, academic and political lecturing, and other formal activities.

The traits and skills that are developed by these kinds of exercises help to close the gap between the native speaker and the non-native speaker/learner. The native speaker does all of these things unconsciously. High-level learners first learn to do these things consciously (at lower levels of proficiency, learners are not even aware of the specifics of the differences) at first, and, with time and practice, they draw ever closer to the unconscious linguistic behavior of the native speaker.

Further Reading

Binder, Carl. 1996. "Behavioral Fluency: Evolution of a New Paradigm." *The Behavior Analyst 19*(2), 163-197.

Davies, Alan. 2003. *The Native Speaker: Myth and Reality.* The Hague: Multilingual Matters.

Gambhihr, Surendra. 2006. "What Does One Need to Get Up to ILR Level 4?" In *Teaching and Learning to Near-Native Levels of Proficiency III: Proceedings of the Fall 2005 Conference of the Coalition of Distinguished Language Centers* (Butler & Zhou). Salinas, CA: MSI Press.

Nair, Kev. 2002. "Speech Generation & Flow Production." Sample pages. Retrieved December 5, 2005 from Adult Faculties Council, Kochi-26 in Kerala, India website: http://www.fluentzy. com/snippet_b2.asp.

Shekhtman, Boris. 2003. *Working with Advanced Foreign Language Learners.* Salinas, CA: MSI Press.

Shekhtman, Boris, & Kupchanka, Dina. 2007. *Communicative Focus.* Salinas: MSI Press.

Shekhtman, Boris, Lord, Natalia, & Kuznetsova, Ekaterina. 2003. "Complication Exercises for Raising the Oral Proficiency Level of Highly Advanced Language Learners." *Journal for Distinguished Language Studies 1* (1): 32-50.

21

Develop Automaticity

Boris Shekhtman
(Specialized Language Training Center)

Superior-level learners already have sufficient automaticity to express their thoughts without thinking about the underlying structure. However, learners at this level, especially the synoptic learners among them, are likely to express thoughts without monitoring structure at all. While they can communicate effectively in this way, they are perceived as learners of the language. Some of these mis-speakings are a matter of making mistakes: they know how to express the thought in a native way, but they do not have the expressions under automatic control. Other of these mis-speakings are due to the fact that involve more rare or complex forms of structure which the learner may not yet have encountered. To reach native-like proficiency, both the common and the rare expressions must be automated. While even native speakers experience slips of the tongue and make careless errors, the errors are different from those of learners, and they do not result from lack of automation or lack of knowledge. They usually come from lack of focus, side thoughts, and other forms of distraction.

The teacher of high-level proficiency courses focuses on bringing the learner to automaticity in four ways. First, he or she encourages learners to spend as much time as possible in the target language environment and to use this environment as a mechanism for language correction and language enrichment. Second, the teacher identifies the structural features that learner has learned but not acquired, i.e., those structures that the learner is using correctly but not automatically. Third, through intensive drilling and the presentation of multiple opportunities for use of the same structural feature in various contexts, the teacher helps the learner to memorize the structure. Fourth, the teacher forces the learner to develop and memorize the essential sophisticated structures that mark a native speaker but remain unfamiliar to the learner, i.e., those structures that he or she is not using at all but rather alternatives that are neither correct nor automatic.

In automatization, the learner is learning to turn declarative memory (knowledge about the language) into procedural memory (performance by habit, like riding a bike). Through many repetitions (yes, "self-drilling," if one wills; drilling is not a curse word, nor even a curse, when it is focused on individualized need for changing the kind of memory being used for language processing), learners can develop the ability to produce an appropriate pattern immediately, correctly, and at the tempo of the native speaker. Repeated exposure and practice are, after all, how native speakers develop automaticity in their own language.

Communicative methods have been accused of developing fluency at the sake of accuracy. Cognitive methods have been accused of the opposite: the development of accuracy at the cost of fluency. An individualized focus on developing automaticity of expression in learners—and this almost always has to be done through skillful diagnosis and subsequent direct instruction—is how teachers of Superior-Distinguished learners help their learners develop both fluency and accuracy, as is needed for native-like language use.

Further Reading

DeKeyser, Richard. 1997. "Beyond Explicit Rule Learning: Automatizing Second Language Morphosyntax." *Studies in Second Language Acquisition 19* (2): 195-222.

Leaver, Betty Lou, & Shekhtman, Boris. 2002. "Principles and Practices in Teaching Superior-Level Language Skills: Not Just More of the Same." In *Developing Professional-Level Language Proficiency* (Leaver & Shekhtman). Cambridge, UK: Cambridge University Press.

Shekhtman, Boris. 2003. "Do Superior-Level Learners Need Language Instruction? An Essay in Answer to the Myth of Natural Acquisition and Self-Study Being Sufficient at High Levels of Foreign Language Acquisition." *ACTR Letter 30* (2): 1-3.

Shekhtman, Boris. 2003. *Working with Advanced Language Learners*. Salinas, CA: MSI Press.

Shekhtman, Boris, 2021. *How to Improve Your Foreign Language Immediately*. Hollister, CA: MSI Press.

22

De-fossilize

Madeline Ehrman
(Foreign Service Institute)

Once world language and cultural behavior is acquired to the level that it is understandable to the native speaker and comfortable enough for the learner to get by with, sophistication in expression and behavior generally stops, i.e., fossilizes. Fossilization of incorrect grammar and lexicon has long been considered a hindrance to learners trying to reach Superior levels of proficiency. Little thought has been given in the professional literature to the concept of fossilization *at* the Superior-level of proficiency, yet fossilization, perhaps more than anything else, is what keeps learners from continuing up the proficiency ladder to native-like professional competency.

Fossilization at the Superior level can occur in several domains. All of these forms of fossilization must be overcome if the Superior-level learner is to reach near-native proficiency. They include functional fossilization, instruction-fostered fossilization, domain-restricted fossilization, affective fossilization, and arrested strategic development.

Functional fossilization refers to the continuing use of inappropriate, inaccurate, or unrefined morphosyntactic and lexical forms by learners who are learning the language as a second language and perhaps in even stronger form by learners who are learning the language as a heritage language. Functional fossilization typically continues unabated since it does not hinder Superior-level learners from communication or task completion unless and until some form of direct instruction breaks down the fossilized errors and replaces them with appropriate forms. Most typically, this occurs by the teacher analyzing the errors and patterns of errors and preparing special drills and opportunities for multiple, frequent, and contextualized use of the correct forms (i.e., natural repetition and practice). In teaching, it is important that teachers use practices that provide learners with limited possibilities to remain in their comfort zones, e.g., by saturating the linguistic environment in the language classroom with new low-frequency grammar and vocabulary, more sophisticated discussions of familiar topics, a wide range of registers, and liberal use of idiomatic expressions.

Instruction-fostered fossilization occurs when teachers try to help learners feel comfortable in language learning. While important at lower levels, this attitude can be counterproductive at higher ones. High-level learners sometimes need to be pushed off their comfortable plateaus if they are to reach a native-like level of proficiency.

Domain-restricted fossilization occurs in Superior-level speech when learners become highly proficient in areas related to their personal lives and work experiences and lose the desire or do not have the opportunity to speak at sophisticated levels about topics in other domains. Some learners may even display native-like language prowess in their very narrow specialty and assume, therefore, that they are at the near-native level. However, Distinguished-level proficiency, by definition, requires breadth, as well as depth. Gaining access to a greater number of domains is one of several reasons why direct instruction can be very important at high levels of proficiency. Teachers can deliberately and planfully take learners into domains that they would not otherwise encounter.

Affective fossilization occurs when learners' self-image and sense of self-efficacy get in the way of continued language improvement. Learners, having reached the Superior level of proficiency, often bask in the compliments they receive from native speaker, not considering that anyone who compliments their proficiency first has to recognize that their language is not that of a native speaker. (Some exceptions might be in cases where physical appearance is such that the observer can tell that the learner is not a native speaker because of hair or skin color, size, and other incongruous attributes.) Language learners at native-like levels of proficiency have recounted being discouraged from seeking higher levels of proficiency when they were at the Superior level because the compliments started turning into complaints: as they became very proficient, they were accepted as native speakers and their mistakes were taken as intentional, causing affront and other kinds of negative reactions from their native-speaker colleagues. Somewhat defective language "protected" them from the higher expectations and judgments that come from being a language user with native-like speech. Developing awareness of this phenomenon is perhaps the easiest way to help learners cope with it: most who encountered it were very surprised and demotivated at first exposure.

Arrested strategic development refers to the tendency to continue to use at higher levels of proficiency the kinds of learning strategies that are more useful at lower levels of proficiency. After spending years getting learners to develop such strategies (e.g., compensation strategies), teachers of high-proficiency learners need to spend weeks and months eliminating such strategies and getting learners to replace them with more appropriate ones for high-level language acquisition.

Most important for the high-level language teacher is to know that fossilization occurs on more than just the level of linguistic forms. Direct instruction with a skilled teacher who has an analytic eye and ear, a strong temperament for driving learners in directions, experience in individualization, and tenacity is often a critical factor in a learner's being able to attain native-like language competence.[9]

Further Reading

Ehrman, Madeline E. 2002. "The Learner at the Superior-Distinguished Threshold." In *Developing Professional-Level Language Proficiency* (Leaver & Shekhtman. Cambridge, UK: Cambridge University Press.

Ehrman, Madeline E. 2002. "Teachers and Learners at the Threshold of Four Level Proficiency." *ACTR Letter 28*(3): 1-3.

Ehrman, Madeline E. 2002. "Understanding the Learner at the Superior/Distinguished Threshold." In *Developing Professional-Level Foreign Language Proficiency* (Leaver & Shekhtman).

Ehrman, Madeline E. 2007. "Understanding Fossilization at High Levels of Foreign Language Proficiency." *Journal for Distinguished Language Studies 4* (forthcoming).

Leaver, Betty Lou. 2003. "Motivation at Native-Like Levels of Foreign-Language Proficiency: A Research Agenda." *Journal for Distinguished Language Studies 1* (1): 59-82.

Shekhtman, Boris, Lord, Natalia, & Kuznetsova, Ekaterina. 2003. "Complication Exercises for Raising the Oral Proficiency Level of Highly Advanced Language Learners." *Journal for Distinguished Language Studies 1* (1): 32-50.

---

[9] This particular categorization of fossilization types was first presented by Madeline Ehrman in Leaver and Shekhtman's edited volume, *Developing Professional-Level Language Proficiency* (Cambridge University Press, 2002).

23

Provide the Appropriate Kind and Quantity of Work

Boris Shekhtman
(Specialized Language Training Center)

Natalia Lord
(Foreign Service Institute)

Svetlana Sibrina
(The George Washington University)

Identification of "appropriate kind and quantity of work" is important for any individualized, learner-centered, and proficiency-oriented program, but it becomes really and truly crucial in the process of designing, developing, and implementing of the so-called short-term project- or task-oriented mini-courses (the authors participated in design, development, and implementation of this type of course during their work at the Specialized Language Training Center [SLTC]). These courses are usually designed for learners who have 3/3+ levels in speaking and reading and listening but need to prepare for specific communicative job-related tasks at a near-native level of proficiency. Below is a generalized description of this type of course.

Short-term project- or task-oriented language mini-courses present an intensive proficiency-oriented content-based language program taught to individual learners or small groups. The individualized, learner-centered, and content-based nature of the courses is reflected in many aspects of the course design, development, and teaching.

The general educational goal of the course is to improve the oral proficiency of a learner in a world language, based on material from a specific professionally oriented topic, by enriching the learner's vocabulary, grammar models, and specific terminology connected with the topic. The usual duration of the course ranges from ten to forty hours of in-class instruction combined with extensive home assignments, including reading, listening, and writing.

The communicative job-related task as the basis and the focus of a course is chosen by the learner. Sometimes, a learner chooses to focus on more than one task. Among the most popular communicative tasks were formal presentations at a conference, interview, negotiation, and discussion.

The instruction for this type of courses is usually provided by one professional instructor although a second and sometimes even a third instructor may be invited on special occasions for specific instructional activities and exercises. Activities with the participation of native speakers are also included in the program. During the course, two or three instructors may work with each individual learner in turn. All instructors are native speakers and professionals in language teaching of Superior-level learners.

These proficiency-oriented courses are taught on the basis of "The Shekhtman Method of Communicative Teaching" (SMCT) (Shekhtman et al., 2002). Like other communicative approaches, SMCT differentiates between language usage and language use, uses goal-oriented teaching that focuses on proficiency outcomes, employs authentic language use in the classroom, assigns authentic tasks, and so on. A detailed description of the methodology appears in "Developing Professional-Level Language Proficiency" (Shekhtman et al., 2002, pp. 119-140).

The type of learning activities and exercises depends on the communicative or learning task and the learner's level of proficiency. All of the individualized courses include the system of communicative exercises developed at the SLTC. The goal of each group of exercises is to master certain communicative sub-goal that is essential for being able to perform the communicative task. The ratio of communicatively oriented to structurally based exercises depends on the level of the learner's accuracy and the knowledge of thematic vocabulary.

As a result of each course being expressly designed for the individual learners based on their professional requirements and current level, the texts and other study materials are chosen with each individual learner in mind and thus the set of texts is updated each time the course is offered. Only authentic language materials are used. The usual package of instructional materials includes:

> 5-10 texts on the chosen professional topic with accompanying pre- and post-reading activities and assignments; in choosing the texts together with each learner, the instructor pays close attention to such considerations as terminological vocabulary enrichment, specific discourse structure, stylistic characteristics of required register, and more personalized aspects of each learner's previously acquired and currently needed proficiency;

> audio and video materials on the chosen professional topic with accompanying pre- and post-listening/watching activities and assignments;

> handouts prepared for conducting various communicative and structural exercises;

> specific assignments based on previous work, with instructions for writing tasks; and

> pertinent and individualized quizzes and tests.

The communicative and structural exercises are chosen based on the observed patterns of mistakes made by the learner. The instructor analyzes these mistakes and chooses appropriate material to eradicate these fossilizations. Commercial textbooks are sometimes used selectively for this type of "remedial" work.

After the course is completed, the learner's performance is evaluated on the ability to function in "real-life communication" and to perform the communicative task selected at the required level of proficiency. This means that by the end of the course, the learner may, for example make a formal presentation before an audience of professionals who are native speakers. The presentation is followed up with a question-and-answer session, and the overall performance is evaluated by the audience. Was the content delivered in form and manner approximating the expected performance of a native speaker who is a specialist in the same field? Does the overall performance meet the ILR Skill Level Description for Level 3+?

The effectiveness of these language courses and their popularity among learners can be explained by the fact that they are designed, developed, and implemented on the basis of "a number of characteristics that differentiate today's cutting-edge programs," i.e., authenticity, content, learner-centered instruction, higher-order thinking, and adult learning... (Leaver, Shekhtman, & Ehrman, 2005, p.14-18). As a result, they are successful in motivating learners and giving them self-confidence in language global proficiency.

Further Reading

Cohen, Bella. 2004. "Diagnostic Assessment at Superior and Distinguished Levels of Proficiency." In *Teaching and Learning to Near-Native Levels of Language Proficiency: The Proceedings of the Spring and Fall 2003 Conferences of the Coalition of Distinguished Language Center*s (Leaver & Shekhtman). Salinas, CA: MSI Press.

Leaver, Betty Lou, & Shekhtman, Boris. 2002. *Developing Professional-Level Language Proficiency.* Cambridge, UK: Cambridge University Press.

Leaver, Betty Lou, & Shekhtman, Boris. 2004. *Teaching and Learning to Near-Native Levels of Second Language Acquisition: Proceedings of the Spring and Fall 2003 Conferences of the Coalition of Distinguished Language Centers.* Salinas, CA: MSI Press.

Leaver, Betty Lou, Shekhtman, Boris, and Ehrman, Madeline. 2005. *Achieving Success in Second Language Acquisition.* Cambridge, UK: Cambridge University Press.

Shekhtman, Boris, & Leaver, Betty Lou with Lord, Natalia, Kuznetsova, Ekaterina, & Ovtcharenko, Elena. 2002. "Developing Professional-Level Oral Proficiency: The Shekhtman Method of Communicative Teaching." In *Developing Professional-Level Foreign Language Proficiency* (Leaver & Shekhtman). Cambridge, UK: Cambridge University Press.

Shekhtman, Boris. 2003. "Do Superior-Level Learners Need Language Instruction? An Essay in Answer to the Myth of Natural Acquisition and Self-Study Being Sufficient at High Levels of Foreign Language Acquisition." ACTR Letter 30 (2): 1-3

24

Choose an Appropriate Approach and Teaching Method

Betty Lou Leaver
(Defense Language Institute Foreign Language Center)

Most current American methods used at lower levels of language proficiency can be successfully used in teaching the superior language learner. During the preparation of learners to talk on a certain topic, for example, we may use the grammar-translation method in reading the text on that topic, analyzing grammar structures of this text and translating some parts of it with the purpose of transferring some elements of the text into the learners' speech. We may use the audio-lingual or direct approach in helping our learners to memorize some expressions which they will need to use in the text of their island. If it is needed, we may augment the cognitive input by offering our learners to listen silently to some tapes connected with the theme of the island to prepare them for deeper understanding of the target grammar and vocabulary. Of course, we, for sure, will use many typical communicative exercises, such as role-plays.

Current language teaching methods are based on the accurate assumption that there is an insurmountable gap between advanced levels of proficiency and those that approximate the proficiency of the native speaker. None of these traditional methods, including communicative ones, intend to bring learners to the native speaker's level; they only intend to improve the given learner's level or at best to push learners closer to a Superior-level command of the language. Indeed, all published language textbooks adapt to the learner's level, which is always lower than that of the native speaker.

Teaching Superior language learners needs new approaches, methods and techniques, which must be based on the principles of the native speaker's performance (Shekhtman & Kupchanka, 2007). It is significantly important to understand the salient elements of a native speaker's communicative manifestations and to turn these elements into the principals of teaching Superior-level learners. For example, in spoken communication, native speakers demonstrate fluency, readiness for any topic, high level of communicative control, and the ability to produce very complicated speech. What are the specific aspects of these elements? How can one use them in teaching Superior-level learners? The answers to these questions are crucial to developing new approaches in teaching Superior-level learners.

Further Reading

Leaver, Betty Lou, & Shekhtman, Boris. 2002. "Principles and Practices in Teaching Superior-Level Language Skills: Not Just More of the Same." In *Developing Professional-Level Language Proficiency* (Leaver & Shekhtman). Cambridge, UK: Cambridge University Press.

Brown, H. Douglas. 2000. *Principles of Language Learning and Teaching*. London: Pearson ESL.

Orwig, Carol J. 1999. "What Is a Language Learning Method?" Retrieved on November 29, 2005 from SIL International Website: http://www.sil.org/lingualinks/ LANGUAGELEARNING/PrepareForLanguageLearning/ WhatIsALanguageLearningMethod.htm

Richards, Jack, & Rogers, Theodore. 2001. *Approaches and Methods in Language Teaching.* Cambridge, UK: Cambridge University Press.

Shekhtman, Boris, & Kupchanka, Dina. 2007. *Communicative Focus: Teaching Foreign Languages on the Basis of Native Speakers' Communicative Focus.* Salinas, CA: MSI Press.

Section IV

Focus on Skills

25

Develop Learners' Ability to Control the Linguistic Interaction

Boris Shekhtman
(Specialized Language Training Center)

Natalia Lord
(Foreign Service Institute)

Svetlana Sirina
(The George Washington University)

Learners' ability to control the linguistic interaction includes the development of skills for entering into a conversation with a native speaker, successfully staying in that conversation, and accomplishing their communicative goals. Controlling the linguistic interaction makes learners equals in communication with native speakers.

The mechanisms ("rules," "tactics," or "devices") can be used at any level of language proficiency because they are adaptable to specific levels. An instructor of high-level language courses must adapt them to the specific level needed.

Perhaps the clearest example of such mechanisms is the "rule of the expanded answer." This rule advises learners to give the most verbose answer possible to the native speakers. This strategy creates an atmosphere of communicative exchange, holds the interest of the native speaker, reduces the amount of (difficult) language directed at the foreigner, limits the language initiative of the native speaker, sets a natural tone for the conversation, and makes the participants in the conversation equal.

Another example is the "island" rule. An "island" is a chunk of language that a learner has fully mastered. For example, native-speaker "islands" that Superior- and Distinguished-level speakers must seek to emulate include formal speeches, lectures, and "opening lines," among other canned segments. The use of such islands helps native speakers to express themselves more precisely and eloquently, and it can do the same for world-language speakers. The language instructor presents islands that are professionally important for Superior-level learners and that contain expressions that are especially useful for them. Automaticity of the island depends on the level of the learner. Generally, the higher the level of the learner, the less important the automaticity of the island. At higher levels, a learner is able to fill in, manipulate, and improvise, as needed. An "island" has several advantages. It prepares the learner for a conversation with a native speaker in advance: the native speaker cannot catch learners off-guard because they are prepared for possible native speaker questions. It instills confidence by putting a very useful tool in their hands and allowing them to feel that the playing field has become more leveled.[10]

Further Reading

Shekhtman, Boris. 2003. *Working with Advanced Foreign Language Learners.* Salinas, CA: MSI Press.

Shekhtman, Boris. 2004. "Profile of an Advanced Learner: Former First Deputy Secretary of State, Strobe Talbott." *Journal for Distinguish Language Studies* 2: 25-26.

[10] The tools described in this article are developed in much greater detail in Shekhtman (2021).

Shekhtman, Boris. 2005. "Two Distinguished Learners— Lawrence Goodrich, Company Director, and Ambassador John Ordway—Partners in Developing an Advanced Program in Foreign Language Instruction." *Journal for Distinguished Language Studies* 3: 15-20.

Shekhtman, Boris. 2021. *How to Improve Your Foreign Language Immediately.* Hollister, CA: MSI Press.

Shekhtman, Boris, Leaver, Betty Lou, & Ehrman, Madeline. 2004. "Questions Typically Asked by Learners in Level 4 Classrooms." In *Teaching and Learning to Near-Native Levels of Language Proficiency: Proceedings of the Spring and Fall 2003 Conferences of the Coalition of Distinguish Language Centers* (Leaver & Shekhtman). Salinas, CA: MSI Press.

Shekhtman, Boris, Lord, Natalia, & Kuznetsova, Ekaterina. 2003. "Complication Exercises for Raising the Oral Proficiency Level of Highly Advanced Learners." *Journal for Distinguished Language Studies 1* (1): 32-59.

Shekhtman, Boris, Lord, Natalia, & Joselyn, Bernardine. 2004. "Demonstration Classroom Exercises." In *Teaching and Learning to Near-Native Levels of Language Proficiency: Proceedings of the Spring and Fall 2003 Conferences of the Coalition of Distinguish Language Centers* (Dubinsky & Butler). Salinas, CA: MSI Press.

26

Expand Learners' Linguistic Repertoire

Rajai Rasheed Al-Khanji
(University of Jordan)

Superior-level learners typically have an excellent theoretical knowledge of all parts of grammar and are able to understand and use a significant amount of vocabulary. Nonetheless, the Superior- level learner is far from the level of a native speaker in many linguistic areas, including depth, breadth, and refinement of vocabulary; unconscious and intuitive grammatical usage, as well as the range of structures, especially in terms of idiolectal, dialectal, and obsolete- but-still-occasionally-used structures; and syntactic variation. It is the possession of this level of linguistic competence, as revealed by fluidity in synonymous expression, that allows the native speaker to readily create and re-create with the language, whether it be for publication, public presentation and debate, research, negotiation, or other sophisticated uses of language that native speakers make on a daily basis.

The language instructor has a difficult assignment to bring the Superior-level learners' linguistic sophistication to this level. This task is complicated because Superior-level learners *control* the grammar system, but native speakers do not need to control it; they just have automatic intuition about this system. Superior-level learners perfectly—and deliberately—control their discourse, but native speakers have a unique capacity to produce fluent spontaneous discourse effortlessly (albeit many native speakers are *not* fluent at producing publishable-quality written language). Superior-level learners have expended much energy over several years, typically as adults, in a classrooms and in-country environment accumulate their vocabulary; native speakers have accumulated a huge memory stock of vocabulary through repeated exposure since birth, as well as literacy work in their school rooms in childhood.

Given this situation, teachers of high-level proficiency courses, when developing learners' speaking skills continue to direct their attention to grammar, with the goal of allowing them to acquire specific and low frequency elements found in texts written for the educated native speaker. It is also important to present with a variety of exercises that train them to express intricate and sophisticated thoughts, using low-frequency grammatical structures. The translation of the texts from the native language of the superior-level learner into the target language is desirable as well.

The actual improvement of lexicon is accomplished through the application of a group of exercises, the goal of which is to develop synonymous expression. Knowledge of synonymous expressions is the basis of lexical richness. A learner, who is capable of giving a full set of synonymous expression for one or another verb or adjective, is distinguished by his self-confidence in his own lexical knowledge and often will beat even a native speaker in this respect.

In L1 education, writing has long been credited with developing learners' language and thinking skills. Besides requiring careful planning, for example, through a formal outline, writing focuses learners' attention on individual words, collocations, idioms, sentence, paragraph and discourse structures. This holds true for writing practice in the L2 as well. In L2 learning and teaching, the practice of writing has several advantages over the practice of speaking in expanding learners' linguistic repertoire.

One of these advantages is the fact that writing is a language activity that any writer can control independently of any interlocutor because writers are also the readers of what they write. And reading what one writes creates a critical distance that allows one to plan and reflect on one's wording, one's choice of words and grammatical structures.

Another advantage of this critical distance created by reading one's own writing is the opportunity to stop the automatized flow of language one has worked so hard to achieve and express oneself with more variation and differentiation. This self-monitoring of the automatized flow of language through reflection on its rhetorical effectiveness provides learners with the opportunity to eliminate Level-3 fossilization by substituting accurate, yet simple language with more complex syntactic patterns and "expanding their range of vocabulary precision and synonymy associated with erudition," as Shekhtman, Lord, and Kuznetsova (2003) have observed.

These processes of planning and critically reflecting on one's writing are, of course, high-level cognitive skills and strategies. Writing thus fosters as much as it benefits from the effective use of L2 learning strategies. As Oxford (1994) observed: "… L2 writing, like L1 writing, benefits from the learning strategies of planning, self-monitoring, deduction and substitution."

The full use of these strategies would be employed in the various stages of the writing process. For the purposes of expanding learners' linguistic repertoire at Level-4, the purpose and audience must clearly indicate the requirement for writing at the Distinguished-level at the outset of any writing assignment. In the prewriting phase, for example, the focus could be on planning the content of the writing task by brainstorming ideas, concepts and associated semantic fields. Here the teacher can seed new vocabulary by offering synonyms for the words and phrases suggested by learners and engaging learners in a discussion of the nuances of meaning differentiating one synonym from another. Learners should then be encouraged to use the new words and phrases in writing a first draft. In revising the first draft, the focus should be on the appropriate use of these new words and phrases. As a next step and before writing a second draft the focus could be shifted to syntactic patterns and considerations of cohesion and coherence. Recommendations made in peer and teacher review and group discussions should then be incorporated in the second draft. Peer and teacher review of the second draft would focus on the effectiveness of both lexical precision and text organization at the sentence, paragraph and discourse levels in achieving the purpose of the written text for the intended audience.

Less holistic learning activities than producing final copy of a high-level writing task are also helpful in expanding learners' linguistic repertoire. For example, asking learners to substitute underlined words and phrases in a model text is a simple, yet effective way to expand learners' vocabulary including synonymous expression. Demands made on the learners can be controlled easily by selecting different model texts.

Encourage learners to experiment with the language. For example, give them fairly narrowly defined writing tasks like narrating an event that is usually related in visual terms through the sense of smell or touch. This will push their creativity and expand their vocabulary. Or have learners describe a person in purely positive and then in purely negative terms. These types of exercises that force writing from an unusual perspective expand learners' vocabulary in playful ways.

In the U.S., textbooks for English composition at the college level are full of ideas about teaching learners at the advanced levels how to expand their linguistic range of expression. There teachers and learners will find suggestions extending from finding just the right word to enriching your expressiveness through figurative speech to varying your sentences in length and structure as well as using inversion, repetition, parallelism

and antithesis for special effects. Making the necessary
adaptations to the peculiarities of their respective L2, teachers
can make these suggestions their own in teaching effective
ways of guiding learners to the linguistic competence required
at the Distinguished level of language proficiency.

Further Reading

Oxford, Rebecca L. 1994. *Language Learning Strategies: An
update.* Washington, D.C.: ERIC Clearing House on Languages
and Linguistics.

Shekhtman, Boris, Lord, Natalia, & Kuznetsova, Ekaterina.
2003. "Complication Exercises for Raising the Oral Proficiency
Level of Highly Advanced Language Learners." *Journal for
Distinguished Language Studies* 1:31-50.

27

Reduce Learners' Accents

Jiaying Howard
(Monterey Institute of International Studies)

Perhaps the most controversial element in defining "native-like" professional proficiency is the role played by accent. The most remarkable example, pointed out time and again by teachers and testers at high levels of language proficiency, is the speech of former U.S. Secretary of State Henry Kissinger. While his erudition exceeds that of even well-educated native speakers and perhaps in his writing he can "pass" for a native speaker, the moment he opens his mouth even the least educated native speaker of English knows that this is a foreigner standing in front of him or her.

Regardless of how impressive other facets of a language user's speech are, a foreign accent will mark that speaker as non-native. Most learners who are striving to reach native-like language proficiency do want to reduce and/or eliminate their foreign accents. Why? Because having an accent marks them as foreign—and then they are often treated as foreign. Because having a strong accent can actually interfere with communication, and even a moderate accent can reduce the amount of comfort the native speaker feels in communicating with the language learner and, hence, the amount of time spent together, the depth of the friendship developed, and the openness that the native speaker is willing to display.

As with ingrained errors in grammar, so, too, ingrained errors in pronunciation have to be identified by a capable language teacher (or speech therapist) and drummed (or drilled) out of the high-level language user. There seem to be no easy solution to this situation. Rather, time spent with a trained phonetician are needed; effort spent not only on pronunciation but also on learning to hear phonemic and allophonic distinctions are important. For some learners (especially auditory ones), being able to hear the distinctions allows them to learn to pronounce them properly. For other learners (especially motor ones), being able to manipulate the oral organs into making the proper sounds can lead to a subsequent ability to make the distinctions auditorily. In the absence of a language laboratory and/ or in addition to it, it is often helpful to have learners record themselves and compare what they say with the speech patterns of a native speaker.

Phonemes are not the only speech feature that highly proficient language users need to get under control. Intonation can be as important, and sometimes more important, than individual sounds. Often, foreigners are misinterpreted (particularly, their tone or mood) because their intonation differs from that of a native speaker, e.g., they use a falling tone (which is interpreted to mean anger or hostility) where a native speaker would use a rising tone. Language laboratory work, as well as in-class work, should focus on bringing learners' intonation in line with the intonational contours of a native speaker. Often, native-like intonation is easier for learners to acquire than are the individual sounds, and in some languages, when intonation is native-like sometimes improperly made sounds are not noticed.

For many years, it has been thought that after the age of puberty, and even in some cases, before it, phonetics were fixed, and new phonemes and allophones could be neither heard nor learned. However, while clearly it *is* significantly more difficult and far less common for adults to learn a language without any or much of a foreign accent, every teacher of Distinguished-level learners with whom we are acquainted has had at least one learner who gives the lie to the assumption, or theory, that it is not possible for adults to approximate a native-sounding accent. Learners who want to lose their accents, are willing to invest the time, and have a knowledgeable coach (teacher or therapist) seem to be able to do so.

Further Reading

Major, Roy. 2002. *Foreign Accent: The Ontogeny and Phylogeny of Second Language Phonology.* Lawrence Erlbaum.

Birdsong, David. 1999. *Second Language Acquisition and the Critical Period Hypothesis.* New Jersey: Lawrence Erlbaum.

Birdsong, David. 1992. "Ultimate Attainment in Second Language Acquisition." *Language 68* (4): 707-755.

28

Build a Deep Understanding of
Culture through Film and Television
and Social Events

Tseng Tseng Chang
(Defense Language Institute Foreign Language Center)

There are many techniques that have been used in teaching world languages. Some techniques are beneficial only for teaching basic-level learners; some are used only in advanced programs; and some are adjustable and depend on the learners' proficiency in the language. The incorporation of films and television into the language-learning program belongs to this category.

If the use of these two devices for Advanced level is, first of all, demonstrative and informative and mainly has a supportive meaning helping learners to improve their comprehension and speaking abilities, the use of them with superior learners is strictly a sociolinguistic phenomenon. Superior learners through films and television begin to cover the gap which culturally divides them from native speakers. That is why the most effective exercises with films are so called "dubbing" or "shadowing" or "echoing" which builds linguistic competence at a higher level of proficiency and which can be characterize as sophisticated form of mimicry.

For example, a learner watches a short clip from a film in which the characters use the combination of complex constructions, idiomatic expressions and specific behaviors typical for the target country. The sound is then turned down as the class watches the clip again. During the second playing, learners attempt to reproduce what they heard the first time. Their goal is to be as accurate and precise as possible while making a full replay of the text. There are several variations that can be done with these kinds of exercise. One such variation is to combine the dubbing activity with practice in translation. In this case, learners translate the difficult constructions during the playback.

The most important exercise, which has the same objective, is when superior-level learners actively participate in this or that social event in the cultural environment of the target country. Here, our learners do two very important things: they communicate with native speakers trying to be equal to them and at the same time absorb all cultural nuances they need. Usually these exercises, if they are the part of the Distinguished-level program, are attentively observed by language instructor, who knows that a learner requires to use curtain number of complicated expressions and memorize some new and important for him/her language and cultural specifics. So, our learner approaches various people, talks with them, asks questions, laughs, explains something to somebody—and fulfills the language instructor's assignment.

Further Reading

Garza, Thomas Jesús. 1996. "The Message is the Medium: Using Video Materials to Facilitate Foreign Language Performance." *Texas Papers in Foreign Language Education* 2(2), 1-18.

Stevick, Earl. 1989. *Success with Foreign Languages: Seven Who Achieved It.* Princeton: Prentice-Hall.

29

Encourage Voracious Reading

James Bernhardt
(Foreign Service Institute)

The most common contribution to reaching high levels of proficiency reported in self-reports by interviewees who possess various world languages at ILR Level 4 and higher is extensive reading—a lot of it. Atwell, for example, a Level-4 learner of English, calls herself a "promiscuous reader."

The Foreign Service Institute, in its Beyond Three programs, takes into account the need for learners to read extensively and the benefits of doing so. In the Beyond Three Russian program, learners are assigned independent reading of novels and equally long literature or documents, a list of which is made, together with the teacher, that takes into account learners' general interests.

Voracious reading is not for the purpose of fluency. It is for the purpose of acquiring sociocultural knowledge, genre, cultural and literary allusions and well-known quotations, etc. Fluency already exists at the Superior-level. There is no need to work on it for the Distinguished-level. In fact, that is the problem that we run into here in the States with new teachers at high levels of proficiency: they assume that they should continue to work on fluency issues as they did at lower levels when what the learners truly need is intensive work on accuracy and precision in both structure and vocabulary. Voracious reading improves both; already being fluent is what allows the voracious reading to be effective.

Further Reading

Leaver, Betty Lou, & Atwell, Sabine. 2002. "Preliminary Qualitative Findings from a Study of the Processes Leading to the Advanced Professional Proficiency Level (ILR 4)" In *Developing Professional-Level Language Proficiency* (Leaver & Shekhtman, eds.). Cambridge, UK: Cambridge University Press.

Leaver, Betty Lou, & Kaplan, Marsha. 2005. "Task-Based Instruction in U. S. Government Slavic Language Programs." In *Task-Based Instruction: Practices and Programs* (Leaver & Willis). Washington, DC: Georgetown University Press.

30

Teach Handwriting

Cornelius Kubler
(Williams College)

Even in this increasingly computerized day and age, most of us in the course of our daily lives has to, at least occasionally, be able to read other people's handwriting. These texts might consist of telephone messages, email messages, letters, receipts, or notes that have been scribbled on the blackboards or whiteboards of lecture halls. Reading handwriting in one's native language can be challenging enough, but in a different world language—especially one with a non-Roman script like Chinese, Japanese, Arabic, or Russian—this ability can be a major source of difficulty. Even the familiar European languages such as French and German have distinct cursive styles and features that differ significantly from American English cursive.

In cursive handwriting, the tip of the writing instrument is lifted from the paper as few times as possible, adjacent strokes being joined for speed and ease of writing, so that what are printed as separate dots and strokes are fused into continuous smooth motions of the brush or pen, since the less often one must pick up the point of one's pen, the faster one can write. This procedure results in a rounding of angles, an increase in the number of interconnected elements, and many more curves and loops than in printing, all of which makes cursive handwriting hard to read. Another reason that cursive handwriting is more difficult to recognize than mechanically produced writing is that there is a greater degree of variation. The factors that may vary include the size of the written symbols, height and width of strokes, relative position of graphic elements, rightward or leftward slant, thickness or thinness of strokes, connected vs. disconnected script, size of loops, presence of artistic flourishes, and amount of spacing between written symbols, words, and lines. Moreover, cursive handwriting frequently includes various abbreviations and simplifications, such as English "sthg" for "something" or "w/o" for "without," as well as borrowings from messaging apps, such as b/c for "because," CU for "See you," etc.

Despite the difficulty, the fact remains that since educated natives possess the ability to read most handwritten documents, non-native learners aiming to achieve native-like competence in another language must also include attaining this ability among their goals. Proficiency in reading cursive handwriting is especially relevant for those living and working overseas, but readers in the

U.S. may also have professional or personal reasons for wishing to read handwritten documents written in another language. The importance and difficulty of reading handwriting are reflected in the Interagency Language Roundtable (ILR) Language Skill Level Descriptions, where there is a gradual progression from (at levels 0+, 1, and 2) recognition and comprehension of typescript only to (at levels 4, 4+, and 5) comprehension of handwriting, including cursive handwriting that is of varying degrees of legibility.

Although there is no substitute for years of practical experience and extensive contact with the native society to become proficient in reading handwriting, direct instruction in class and work with specially prepared training materials can significantly speed up the learning process. Advanced-level instructors and learners should ensure that among the reading texts used, there is sufficient variety not only in linguistic content (e.g., vocabulary, grammar, and discourse organization) but also in written form (e.g., typeface, print size, and styles of handwriting).

In an advanced training program, learners should periodically have the opportunity to work with handwritten documents, progressing from relatively legible to relatively illegible. The main objective should be reading recognition, not writing ability, which is a more difficult skill to develop and which, in any case, is of more limited utility to language learners. However, for the purpose of promoting reading recognition, learners may occasionally be asked to copy certain high-frequency cursive forms.

The instructor should provide learners with background information on the history of the writing system, including cursive forms both past and present. Detailed information on how individual strokes and components of the writing system are written in common cursive styles should be provided. While such explanation can be useful for learners, even more important is copious practice in reading texts handwritten by a variety of different writers.

One useful strategy is first to present a document in the original cursive form and ask learners to try to read it in class (or have learners read it on their own at home). The instructor can then present learners with the same text in printed-style handwriting or typescript for them to compare with the cursive version. Special problems and areas of difficulty should be pointed out and any questions that learners may have can be addressed. It is essential that exercises that help learners practice the new material and require them to perform assigned tasks be included. Learners can be asked to read passages in cursive handwriting and find out certain types of information; or they can be asked to answer questions on the content of a passage, rewrite a passage in printed-style handwriting, summarize a passage orally in the world language, or translate it into English. One particular problem in recognizing cursive handwriting is that a single cursive form can sometimes represent more than one word or element of the writing system. For this reason, learners must be trained always to make careful use of the context.

Textbooks on recognition of cursive handwriting designed for non-native learners are available for some languages; for other languages, there may be orthography manuals and related materials for native learners that can be adopted for use by non-native learners. Instructors may also wish to prepare their own materials. In that case, it is important that the writing samples they provide not all be written by themselves, but also include a wide range of materials written by many different writers of varying educational background, gender, and age. Both instructors and learners should constantly be on the lookout for handwritten texts that they may encounter in their daily lives, grading and filing them for future use by degree of difficulty. Such authentic materials can be invaluable for personal study, teaching, and the preparation of training materials in reading handwriting designed for others.

Further Reading

Kubler, Cornelius C. 2002. "Learning Chinese in China: Programs for Developing Superior-to-Distinguished-Level Chinese Language Proficiency in China and Taiwan." In *Developing Professional- Level Language Proficiency* (Leaver & Shekhtman). Cambridge, UK: Cambridge University Press.

Kubler, Cornelius C. 2005. "Developing Learners' Proficiency in Reading Cursive Handwriting". In *Teaching and Learning to Near-Native Levels of Language Proficiency: Proceedings of the Fall 2004 Conference of the Coalition of Distinguished Language Centers* (Dubinsky & Robin). Salinas, California: MSI Press.

Kubler, Cornelius C. 2005. "The Handwriting is on the Wall, But Can We Read it? Training Superior-to-Distinguished-Level Learners in the Recognition of Cursive Handwriting." *Journal for Distinguished Language Studies* 3:27-40.

31

Teach Music and through Music

Michael Morrisey
(University of Kassel, Germany)

In teaching music, many activities can be used at Level 4 that are used at lower levels, but the orientation is significantly different. Folk songs, for example, are usually associated with the elementary stages of language learning and young learners, but they can also be a rich source of cultural, historical, and linguistic enrichment for adults.

Only a minority of folk songs are children's songs. Most have serious themes which preserve not so much the facts of history as the voices of the people who lived it. In one of the most famous, and often heard, songs of the Famine, "Skibbereen," a father tells his son of their eviction from their land because he could not pay the rent, of the death of his wife after the eviction, and of his subsequent involvement in revolutionary activities. Like many songs written by exiles in America, this one ends with the hope of someday returning with an army of Fenians to free the homeland.

Almost every line of the song offers opportunities to discuss and expatiate upon the historical and cultural context, as well as the linguistic features of the text itself. Level-4 learners are able, and should be encouraged, to do this research themselves, by using a wide variety of the same kinds of resources that native speaker learners would use in analyzing such songs in literature classes: critical analyses, literary criticism books, genre histories, specialty dictionaries, etymological studies, and the like.

In a lighter vein, songs can challenge not only the learner's historical and cultural understanding but also his or her articulatory apparatus. In one version of "The Bold O'Donoghue," the singer(s) is called upon to imitate, in jocular fashion, various contemporary English accents.

Although professional singers can sometimes imitate native-like pronunciation in a world language, this takes a lot of practice and is generally limited to a particular song. It is not a skill they can apply spontaneously. A Level-4 speaker, however—provided s/he has a taste for singing—can often hear, reproduce, and create the same kind of subtle and spontaneous modulations of voice that come naturally to native speakers, both in singing and in normal speech.

Further Reading

Morrissey, Michael. 2001. *Song and Story: An Anthology of Irish Folk Songs.* Books on Demand.

32

Teach Dialects

Cornelius Kubler
(Williams College)

Most languages of the world have both standard forms, which are the kind usually taught to foreigners, and dialects, which may be spoken by sizeable populations of native speakers. There may also be speakers who attempt to speak the standard form but speak it imperfectly due to influence from their native dialect, with non-standard pronunciation, vocabulary, and grammar.

Educated native speakers of a language typically understand the general meaning of speech in commonly encountered dialects of their language. For example, native speakers of American English would be able to understand the majority of the English spoken in the American deep South or in England and educated native speakers of French would be able to understand most speech in the French of Brittany or Provence. Therefore, non-native learners aiming to reach native-like levels of language competence must also be able to understand the gist of speech in the common dialects of a language.

The importance and difficulty of understanding dialects are reflected in the Interagency Language Roundtable (ILR) Language Skill Level Descriptions, where there is a gradual progression from (at Levels 3 and below) no comprehension of dialects to (at Levels 3+ and 4) comprehension of the essentials of speech in some major dialects to (at Levels 4+ and 5) full comprehension of all speech that would be intelligible to a well-educated native speaker, even in a number of "regional" and "illiterate" or "extreme" dialects.

Currently, in their U.S. language classrooms, learners are typically exposed only to the relatively standard speech of their instructors and are not accustomed to hearing non-standard accents and usages. This is one reason why, for many of the thousands of Americans who travel overseas each year, communication falters on their first arrival in country. Ironically, the learners we now produce are not infrequently better in speaking than in comprehension; that is, they can often make themselves understood to native speakers but may not comprehend what native speakers are saying to them. Certainly, use of non-standard speech is not the only reason for this, but it is a major factor.

Language learners should be made aware early in their study of a language that dialectal differences exist, and they should occasionally be exposed to easy non-standard speech once they attain approximately Level 2. Exposure to dialects earlier than that might confuse them and could interfere with their learning of the standard language. About the time that learners reach Level 3 to 3+, or immediately preceding (or in conjunction with) in-country study, they should be given detailed instruction in listening comprehension of dialects and dialect-influenced non-standard speech.

Though it is true that, to become really proficient in listening comprehension of dialects, there is no substitute for living and traveling widely in the country for a period of years, there are numerous strategies and shortcuts that can be explicitly taught in class so as to make learners' learning proceed more efficiently. To help learners develop their listening comprehension of different varieties of a language, we recommend that the instructor should:

1. Present learners with an overview of the general dialect situation in the country or countries using the language, including information on the background and distribution of the major dialects;

2. Provide learners with detailed information on the linguistic features of the major dialects and dialect-influenced non-standard speech varieties, contrasting them with the standard language in pronunciation, vocabulary, and grammar. If possible, the instructor should play audio recordings of several common dialects so that learners can begin to develop a "feel" for them. Teach strategies and shortcuts, e.g., that a certain sound or class of sounds in a non-standard variety corresponds to a certain sound or class of sounds in the standard language.

3. Invite speakers of the major dialects and non-standard speech varieties to come to class to give informal talks to the learners about their families, professions, daily lives, etc. The speakers should hail from all walks of life, since there are likely to be substantial differences from one speaker to the next depending on sociolinguistic factors such as level of education, age, and urban vs. rural upbringing. After each talk, which should be recorded for later reference, learners should be encouraged to ask the speaker as many questions as possible.

4. At the next class session, instructor and learners should systematically go over the recording of the speaker's presentation, with the instructor explaining difficult parts and converting (or asking learners to convert) into standard speech all the non-standard usages. Learners should be allowed access to the recording and should be required, in the language lab or at home, to listen to the recording several more

times and answer questions or perform other exercises based on it to be handed in at the next class session.

5. Include listening comprehension of dialects and dialect-influenced speech on tests and exams. For group tests, a brief recorded passage can be played, with learners instructed to answer questions based on it or sum up the main points of the passage in English. For individual tests, learners can be presented with a tape recorder containing a tape of several short passages recorded in the dialects that have been studied. Learners can then be asked to interpret into the standard language, or into English, the gist of what the speaker says. Learners may be allowed to rewind and replay each section as many times as needed, with the examiner noting down the number of replays each learner requires as well as the accuracy of the interpretations.

In addition to improving listening comprehension, training such as that described above has the additional benefits of increasing learners' knowledge of the society and culture, developing their ability to identify a speaker's place of origin from listening to her or his speech, and strengthening their overall language proficiency by expanding their vocabulary and grammar. While developing speaking proficiency in dialects is not included among the training objectives, if the learner happens to pick up a few common phrases in several major dialects, this can certainly be useful and enhance her or his credibility in the world society.

Further Reading

Kubler, Cornelius C., & Ho, George T. C. 1984. *Varieties of Spoken Standard Chinese, Volume II: A Speaker from Taipei.* Dordrecht, Holland: Foris Publications.

Kubler, Cornelius C. 2002. "Learning Chinese in China: Programs for Developing Superior-to-Distinguished-Level Chinese Language Proficiency in China and Taiwan." In *Developing Professional- Level Language Proficiency* (Leaver & Shekhtman). Cambridge University Press, 96-118.

Kubler, Cornelius C. 2003. "Developing Superior-to-Distinguished- Level Learners' Listening Comprehension of Dialects and Dialect-Influenced Non-Standard Speech." *Journal for Distinguished Language Studies* 1:7-19.

33

Moving from the Concrete to the Abstract: A Superior-Level Speaking Task

Orlando Kelm
University of Texas at Austin

As speakers progress from Intermediate and Advanced levels of proficiency to Superior levels, one of the greatest challenges is to move away from exclusively talking about oneself, solely giving personal examples, or merely sharing personal anecdotes. Superior levels of proficiency imply an ability to defend "concrete and abstract" perspectives. This means that Superior-level speakers should be able to structure both sides of an argument and not simply repeat their own personal opinions about a given topic.

My experience is that sometimes, even when speakers have the ability, accuracy, and fluency to be Superior-level speakers, they still fail to achieve Superior-level scores during an Oral Proficiency Interview. This is because learners have a tendency to only express personal opinions and individual perspectives.[11] We need to assist learners to become aware of strategies that move beyond the expression of self.

When speakers only give references to their own experience, there is a tendency to remain with "concrete" topics. Notice that Advanced-level speakers tell first-person accounts, stories,

---

[11] This is what Madeline Ehrman (2002) refers to as level fossilization: the comfort of the familiar winning out over the fear of the unfamiliar.

and examples (*This happened to me once when... I believe this is important because... One time I was in Rio when I saw...*) The challenge for Superior-level speakers is to demonstrate an ability to discuss abstract thought (which requires more sophisticated and complex language). Notice in the examples below that Superior-level tasks are frequently presented as a dichotomy. Superior-level speakers demonstrate an ability to discuss the pros and cons of both sides of the argument, the issue, or the problem:

- Some people say face-to-face classes are more effective, others say virtual classes are better.
- Some people say a structured management style is more effective, others say that a free-style approach is better.
- Some people say that working from home is advantageous, others say that coming together at the office is better.
- Some people say that gasoline cars are more efficient, and others say that alternative energy cars have a bright future.
- Some people say that security at airports is necessary to protect passengers, while others say that moving people along efficiently and quickly is a priority.
- Some say that family structure should focus on small nuclear networks, while others believe that large extended family enhances quality.
- Some say that sports and politics should be separate, and others think that sports figures have every right to use their position and influence for awareness and change.

There is some irony to the challenge of asking learners NOT to give their own opinion about a given topic because normally we are pushing them to express opinions. But as a Superior task, putting personal opinions off-limits forces speakers to consider both sides of an argument. One of the characteristics of Superior-level speech is to move beyond the "what is" and enter into the world of "what if." Again, this causes a speaker to consider conjecture, hypothesis, and possible outcomes.

With all of this in mind, here is how we structure Superior-level tasks for our learners:

1. Compare both sides of a given argument and express the pros and cons of each.

2. Discuss the implications of what would happen by following through with each

3. side of the argument.

4. Identify how opposing sides of an issue might respond or challenge a given stand

5. or opinion.

6. If you do express a personal opinion, do so only within the context of

7. strengthening a point of view.

Further Reading

Ehrman, Madeline E. 2002. "The Learner at the Superior-Distinguished Threshold." In *Developing Professional Level Language Proficiency* (Leaver & Shekhtman). Cambridge, UK: Cambridge University Press.

Swender, Elvira and Robert Vicars (eds). 2012. ACTFL: Oral Proficiency Interview Tester Training Manual. Alexandria, VA: ACTFL.

34

Two Words Are Better Than One: The Importance of Collocations in Learners' Vocabularies

Maria Shardakova
(Indiana University)

Superior-level L2 users are expected to communicate effectively across various discourses in diverse social settings, while producing and comprehending a broad variety of text types. Such efficiency and flexibility require a good command of L2 vocabulary. Indeed, empirical studies show that knowledge of L2 vocabulary accounts for 37-62% of the variance in language proficiency (Alderson, 2005), with both productive and receptive L2 skills improving with increases in vocabulary (speaking: Hilton, 2008; writing: Laufer & Nation, 1995; reading: Laufer & Ravenhorst-Kalovski, 2010; and listening: van Zeeland & Schmitt, 2013).

In addition to the size of vocabulary, researchers have stressed the importance of formulaic and patterned language (for a review see Gablasova, Brezina, & McEnery, 2017), arguing that the ability to communicate fluently and effortlessly, in a nativelike manner, in real time hinges on the knowledge of prefabricated chunks that vary in the degree of fixedness from lexically bound idioms (*in the blink of an eye*) to more open combinations that usually co-occur in speech (*break a promise*) (Ellis et al., 2015). While collocations are pervasive in language, helping speakers expedite and enhance communication, frame experiences, organize texts, and express identity (Wray, 2002), they also present a serious challenge even for advanced learners (Erman et al., 2016) and thus require pedagogical mediation.[12]

To help learners master collocations, the following techniques, born out of classroom practice and informed by vocabulary research, can be suggested. These techniques draw on both implicit and explicit learning.

First, when selecting instructional materials, instructors can apply the narrow reading and listening approach in order to increase the frequency of occurrence of target collocations and to stimulate incidental learning. (Such an approach is especially effective for the modular curriculum that promotes focused instruction within a teaching unit). With collocations being as susceptible to incidental learning as individual words (Chang, 2019), instructors are advised to follow Schmitt's (2010) estimate postulating that learners develop a passive knowledge of a word after 8-10 occurrences in input. Since different discourses and text types use predictable sets of collocations, selecting materials that address the same topic (e.g., climate change), come from the same type of discourse (e.g., academic), and represent a particular text type (e.g., research article) increases exposure to target collocations and promotes learning. To help leaners notice (Schmidt, 1990) target collocations in input, instructors can use various techniques, such as glossing or highlighting. If necessary, authentic texts can be further modified to increase the frequency of a collocation's occurrence and showcase variations. For instance, to expose learners to variations of a collocation – *address the*

---

[12] This conclusion by researchers observing learner needs is further supported by a survey of more than 100 professional language users with Distinguished-level proficiency, the vast majority of which (75%) stated that the needed instruction to reach Level 4 and still desired instruction at Level 4 because the nuances of language at the level often lay out of reach of the language learners' intuitions, deductions, and experiences (Leaver & Atwell, 2002).

question, raise the question, put forward the question – the instructor can manipulate the existing collocations or add new examples.

Second, instructors can incorporate awareness-raising activities to help learners discover the underlying structure of collocations, understand their functions, and expand repertoires through syntactic synonymity. It has been demonstrated that different types of collocations are acquired at different rates and with varying accuracy. For example, research shows that learners are more successful in acquiring collocations that have L1 equivalents or those with transparent structure rather than unique culture-specific collocations with opaque internal structure (González & Ramos, 2013). To alert learners to these differences, they can be assigned to search for collocations in a given printed or audio-text, categorize collocations based on their transparency, and explain their meaning by consulting dictionaries.

When categorizing collocations, particular attention should be paid to expressions that provide structure and navigation to various text types. For instance, an academic argument in Russian is often shaped by the following sequentially arranged expressions: *dannaia rabota posviashchena teme, rassmatrivaiutsia raznye podkhody, s odnoi storony, s drugoi storony, eto pozvoliaet zakluchit', chto.* "If learners internalize these phrases, they will be able to effectively express a position on any topic, while freeing up their working memory to focus on domain-specific vocabulary and structures in order to deliver well-formed and topic-relevant arguments.

Another important category of collocations includes those performing specific rhetorical functions, such as comparisons, hyperboles, emphatic constructions, appeals, rhetorical questions, to name just a few. These expressions are particularly useful for constructing the speaker/writer's identity and can be easily recycled across a variety of text types.

In addition to learning collocations that organize texts (discourse-framing collocations) or express one's stance (rhetorical devices), learners should be encouraged to expand their knowledge of collocational variations and syntactical synonyms of collocations. The ability to manipulate collocations paradigmatically (*ask a question, raise a question, put forward a question*) and syntagmatically (*ask a question, address an issue, inquire*) will enrich learners' speech and help them adapt to diverse communicative contexts.

A useful strategy that instructors can teach their learners is constructing individual electronic collocational databases. Organized by topic, text type, function, and main word, these e-vocabularies will come in handy for writing assignments and oral presentations. Eventually internalized through rehearsed performance, these individually selected collocations will become a part of learners' spontaneous repertoire.

Third, when designing tasks for productive use of collocations, instructors should incorporate activities with controlled production (e.g., gap-filling) as such activities promote longer-lasting gains compared to open-ended tasks (Vyatkina, 2016). These controlled-production activities can incorporate individual collocations or sequences of collocations that organize a particular text type. For instance, with an earlier example of Russian collocations employed in argumentative discourse, learners can be prompted to put collocations in order or supply missing items to sequentially organized collocations. For open-ended production, instructors can ask learners to incorporate a particular number ("use at least five collocations") or type of collocations ("use collocations for text navigation," "use emphatic collocations to express righteous indignation").

Further, to sensitize learners to patterned language, instructors can take advantage of technology and the growing number of language corpora. Learners who know how to use electronic corpora to self-correct can expand their knowledge of collocations.

Any combination of these strategies will enhance learners' vocabularies; however, used together, these strategies will guide the process of collocation learning in its entirety from input selection and enhancement to awareness-raising activities and ultimately production. The purpose is not only to enrich learners' current vocabularies but also to provide learners with tools and techniques to become life-long autonomous learners.

Further Reading

Alderson, J. Charles. 2005. *Diagnosing Foreign Language Proficiency: The Interface between Learning and Assessment.* London: Continuum.

Chang, Anna C-S. 2019. "Effects of Narrow Reading and Listening on L2 Vocabulary Learning." *Studies in Second Language Acquisition, 41,* 769-794.

Ellis, Nick C., Simpson-Vlach, Rita, Römer, Ute, O'Donnell, Mathew B., & Wulff, Stephanie. 2015. *Learner Corpora and Formulaic Language in Second Language Acquisition Research.* Cambridge, UK: Cambridge University Press.

Erman, Britt, Forsberg Lundell, Fanny F., & Lewis, Margarita. 2016. "Formulaic Language in Advanced Second Language Acquisition and Use." In *Advanced Proficiency and Exceptional Ability in Second Languages* (Hylstenstam). Boston, MA: De Gruyter Mouton.

Gablasova, Dana, Brezina, Vaclav & McEnery, Tony. 2017. "Collocations in Corpus-based Language Learning Research: Identifying, Comparing, and Interpreting the Evidence." *Language Learning, 67,* 155–179.

González, A. Orol., & Ramos, M. Alonso. 2013. "A Comparative Study of Collocations in a Native Corpus and a Learner Corpus of Spanish." *Procedia-Social and Behavioral Sciences 95*: 563-570.

Hilton, Heather. 2008. "The Link between Vocabulary Knowledge and Spoken L2 Fluency." *The Language Learning Journal 36*: 153-166.

Laufer, Batia, & Ravenhorst-Kalovski, Geke C. 2010. "Lexical Threshold Revisited: Lexical Text Coverage, Learners' Vocabulary Size and Reading Comprehension. *Reading in a Foreign Language 22*:15-30.

Laufer, Batia, & Nation, Paul. 1995. "Vocabulary Size and Use: Lexical Richness in L2 Written Production." *Applied Linguistics 16*: 307-322.

Leaver, Betty Lou, & Atwell, Sabine. 2002. "Preliminary Qualitative Findings from a Study of the Processes Leading to the Advanced Professional Proficiency Level (ILR 4)" In *Developing Professional-Level Language Proficiency* (Leaver & Shekhtman, eds.). Cambridge, UK: Cambridge University Press.

Schmidt, Richard. 1990. "The Role of Consciousness in Second Language Learning." *Applied Linguistics 11*: 129-158.

Schmitt, Norbert. 2010. *Researching Vocabulary: A Vocabulary Research Manual*. London: Springer.

Van Zeeland, Hilde, & Schmitt, Norbert. 2012. "Lexical Coverage in L1 and L2 Listening Comprehension: The Same or Different from Reading Comprehension?" *Applied Linguistics 34*: 457-479.

Vyatkina, Nina. 2016. "Data-Driven Learning of Collocations: Learner Performance, Proficiency, and Perceptions." *Language Learning & Technology 20*: 159-179.

Wray, Alison. (2002). *Formulaic language and the lexicon.* Cambridge University Press.

Thomas Jesús Garza, Ed. D.

35

Using Authentic Materials for Cultural Journals and Oral Presentations

Vivian Flanzer
(University of Texas at Austin)

For a successful and positive intercultural communication, language learners need not only to hone their language skills but also their cross-cultural knowledge. This knowledge about how to interact appropriately in different contexts and with people from different backgrounds is acquired thorough self-reflection and the contextual analysis of the target language and the target culture.

At the Superior level, language learners have the ability to examine the products, practices and perspectives of the target culture critically and without judgment. In addition, they can fully participate in informal spoken and written discussions and formal academic oral and written presentations about a wide range of topics to a varied audience.

Language educators have long endorsed the benefits of using teaching materials based on authentic resources—written by native speakers for a native speaker audience—as they enable learners to acquire the target language in the context of a culture's ideas, values and practices. Whereas the contrived materials of language textbooks may present learners with a rarefied and distorted sample of the target language, authentic materials such as videos, commercials, and different reading genres offer a richer source of input to develop learners' communicative competence. Audio-visual materials in particular can enable learners to travel to the target country without leaving the classroom, thereby increasing their abilities to make cultural comparisons and gain insights into the target culture. The combination of authentic media (for example, screening of a video based on a reading) increases learners' motivation and comprehension of the target language and culture.

In order to help my Intermediate-level Portuguese students to move toward Superior language and cross-cultural proficiency, I incorporate in my classes the writing of cultural journals and oral cultural presentations and debates, based on authentic materials. These materials can be accessed through *ClicaBrasil*, an Open Educational Resource developed to teach the Portuguese language and Brazilian culture to intermediate and advanced language learners. *ClicaBrasil* contains several culturally rich authentic literary texts (e.g., song lyrics, magazine articles, and short stories) and 157 authentic and non-scripted videos of Brazilians from all regions and sectors of society speaking spontaneously about their lives, their country, and topics that arise from these readings, enabling learners not only to experience the language as "lived" by native speakers in Brazil but also to grasp the sociocultural context of the readings through their testimonies. The authentic videos and readings are integrated with hundreds of activities that hone language skills - reading, grammar, vocabulary, writing, listening and reading comprehension, oral competence—through exposure to Brazilian culture as well as guiding questions that prompt discussions and reflections on cross-cultural knowledge and competence.

Learners compose several cultural journals, in which they write, in academic style, about their observations and reflections regarding the Portuguese language and Brazilian culture they perceived while interacting with the aforementioned authentic videos and readings. Some of the topics they write about include what was chosen to be said by the speakers (and what was left unsaid); gestures and non-verbal communication; words, verbs, or expressions that are used differently in written and oral Portuguese; interesting ways that these different Brazilians use grammar or pronounce words differently; and anything that they find interesting, intriguing, different or similar to their language and culture. Learners are instructed to back up their reflections with concrete examples from the authentic materials and to incorporate the complex grammar structures and the new vocabulary they learned in class and through the authentic materials into their written production.

After correcting each journal and giving individual feedback to each student, I copy/paste anonymous sentences from the journals that represent the most common linguistic challenges that would be worthy reviewing as a class. In small groups, learners are asked to rewrite these sentences, correcting what seems necessary. Afterwards, each group presents their sentences in a class discussion. This collaborative activity reviews the group's most difficult challenges and encourages different points of view and forms of expressions, as often there are different ways of communicating the same ideas.

In a subsequent class, learners are given one minute to present orally to the class the observations and reflections they wrote about in their journals. In preparation for their presentations, they are instructed to summarize the main points of their arguments, and to logically combine the examples to illustrate and justify it. The presentations are followed by a class debate, in which learners expand on their reflections as they dialogue with their peers (agreeing or disagreeing).

Through these exercises, learners appreciate the complexities of learning a language through enticing multimodal authentic materials (such as videos and literary readings) and tasks that prompt them to understand and produce the Portuguese language, at the same time as they reflect upon and deepen their knowledge of Brazilian society. They also learn about sociolinguistics variation, and that language use is not homogeneous, being influenced by social factors, such as region, class, age, and gender, and the context of the interaction. This way, learners are not only understanding Portuguese and about key issues about Brazilian society, but, most important, they are learning to analyze language in context, and to think critically about language use and society. These exercises in the target language inevitably prompt self-reflection and the discovery of unconscious aspects of their own language use, enabling them to make realizations about their lives and identities. It also promotes diversity and inclusion by fostering respect and tolerance toward the peoples and ideas we are studying about and the deconstruction of stereotypes.

Further Reading

Al Azri, Rashid Hamed, & Al-Rashdi, Majid Hilal. 2014. "The Effect of Using Authentic Materials in Teaching." *International Journal of Scientific and Technology Research 3(10)*: 249-354.

Johnson, Stacey Margarita. 2021. "Authentic Resources and Written Reflection as Contributors to Transformative Learning." In *Transformative Language Learning and Teaching* (Leaver, Davidson, & Campbell). Cambridge, UK: Cambridge University Press.

36

Focus on High-Level Listening

Karen Evans-Romaine
(University of Wisconsin-Madison)

Listening at all proficiency levels presents particular complications for interpretation: speech rate, word boundaries, qualities of spontaneous speech (repetition, false starts, restatements, hesitations and pauses, and other facets of what Brown and Lee call "performance variables"), acoustics, and challenges specific to short-term memory. Unlike in reading, in which one can reread what is at first difficult to interpret, often we hear spoken discourse only once, without the possibility of repetition: a live public speech, a congratulatory toast, a public service announcement, rapid-fire directions in an emergency. Listening at high levels of proficiency includes all of these variables and adds the greater challenges of text types with a high cognitive load (interviews, arguments, debates, lectures and other forms of high-level public discourse, newscasts on complex topics), register range (from highly colloquial to highly sophisticated speech), and lexical precision, in which nuances of meaning could affect our interpretation and response to a particular utterance.

Because of the variety of challenges, instruction in listening requires activation of both "top-down" and "bottom-up" strategies and of focus on both breadth and depth, alternating in assignments between close attention to a short audio or video segment and exposure of students to a great deal and a wide variety of speech samples, varying by genre, text type, register, dialect and idiolect.

In a course on listening and speaking at the Advanced and Superior levels focused on current events and media, one useful approach to take is to follow several speakers across a variety of genres throughout the course to observe and analyze the speech patterns, vocabulary, and rhetorical devices of several speakers across a variety of text or speech types from a public speech, in which the text has been prepared in advance and for which a transcript is available, to a press conference, an interview, and an excerpt from a news report including spontaneous speech. From these samples one can create exercises based on rhetorical devices repeated by one speaker in several different speech contexts in order to teach students to recognize them and to recreate their own utterances using them in order to help retain them and to expand learners' vocabulary. Such exercises can be created from speech openings, responses to questions in an interview, ways in which the speaker both interrupts and stops interruptions, ways in which the speaker defends or opposes a point of view, ways in which the speaker changes the subject. These rhetorical "islands" (Shekhtman, 2002) can be adapted to help students develop Superior-level discourse in high-stakes genres such as public speeches, press conferences, debates, and interviews. Transcripts can be used in order to help learners distinguish word borders and develop vocabulary, as aids to comprehension if presented in advance, or for comprehension self-checks if presented after a lesson. For small segments, students can be tasked to create their own transcripts and can then check them against transcripts presented after the assignment; this form of dictation at higher levels of proficiency can help develop vocabulary and the ability to distinguish word boundaries.

Another useful genre for teaching listening is documentary film, which has several advantages: it tells a story which listeners can be asked to retell, it includes a variety of speakers and thus a variety of speech features ("performance variables"), and it can provide the basis for deeper analysis of a biographical, literary, political, or historical topic. In addition, documentary film lends itself to both "macro" or "top-down" and "micro" or "bottom-up" approaches. Among "top-down" assignments, students can be asked to retell scenes from the film (usually an Advanced-level skill), to represent the points of view of various speakers on one topic (a character, event, or issue depicted or discussed in the film; a Superior-level skill), and can be assigned other works on the same topic and asked to compare them. Among "bottom-up" tasks, in-class instruction can focus on specific, short scenes in order to teach students to determine word and phrase boundaries; focus on the semantics of word order; focus on lexical nuances, including synonyms, euphemisms, circumlocutions; and on pragmatics, such as avoidance strategies, argumentation strategies, interruption strategies or those to prevent interruption. Learners can be taught Superior-level vocabulary and Distinguished-level stylistic references, register differences, and lexical and rhetorical nuances by such focused, "micro-level" listening. An alternation in focus between "macro-level" and "micro-level" tasks teaches students learning strategies specific to listening: to focus on the gist of an argument heard only once or twice and to be able to reformulate that argument or an opposite argument—skills necessary in debate and negotiations; to focus on word choice while developing synonyms and an understanding of their semantic and pragmatic differences; to listen for rhetorical devices and the ways in which they convey points of view.

The advantage of teaching listening in a digital age is that many learners spend a great deal of their time on listening for meaning through audio or video news reports, podcasts, and various entertainment genres. The instructor at the Superior and Distinguished levels can harness the strategies learners use for listening in their own language and help focus students' attention on strategies needed for listening in another language.

Further Reading

Brown, H. Douglas, & Lee, Heekyeong. 2015. *Teaching by Principles: An Interactive Approach to Language Pedagogy.* 4th ed. White Plains, NY: Pearson.

Shekhtman, Boris, & Leaver, Betty Lou, with Lord, Natalia, Kuznetsova, Ekaterina, & Ovtcharenko, Elena. 2002. "Developing Professional-Level Oral Proficiency: The Shekhtman Method of Communicative Teaching." In *Developing Professional-Level Language Proficiency* (Leaver & Shekhtman). Cambridge University Press. 119-140.

Section V

Focus on Assessment

Section V

Focus on Assessment

37

Conduct Periodic
Diagnostic Assessment

Betty Lou Leaver
(Defense Language Institute Foreign Language Center)

Successful language programs providing instruction at the Superior and Distinguished levels (e.g., the advanced Russian course at the Foreign Service Institute (FSI), which began in 1984) have, for years, used diagnostic assessment as a mechanism for determining how best to shape and individualize instruction. Most of the US government language schools now routinely conduct diagnostic assessments for many, if not most, of their learners as a way of making instruction the most efficient possible, as well as effective. Diagnostic assessment has also been used for a long time in successful private world-language programs aimed at helping learners reach native- like proficiency (e.g., at the Specialized Language Center [SLTC] in Rockville, Maryland).

In the early 1990s, the Defense Language Institute Foreign Language Center (DLIFLC) used recall protocols as a way of attempting to determine strengths and weaknesses in receptive skills and then developed lessons to shore up the weaknesses in individual learners. Since those days, the DLI has made many strides forward in diagnosis. In the early 2000s, "can-do" statements, later used by other organizations and programs (e.g., the LangNet self-leveling questions), to help learners self-assess their proficiency level, along with strengths and weak- nesses within a level. In very recent years, the DLI has developed the Diagnostic Assessment process into a formal tool that is used with military language programs worldwide. The tools that they use include a learning styles test, a four-skills interview, a follow-up counseling session, and an individualized learning plan. The Directorate of Continuing Education where the Diagnostic Assessors are currently assigned has prepared Diagnostic Kits—packets of reading and listening materials, samples of learning plans, instructions to assessors, and the like.

Expanding upon diagnostic assessments used in the Russian and Asian & African Sections in the early 1980s, in 1989, the Foreign Service Institute established a new directorate: Research, Evaluation, and Development. One of the innovations of this directorate was the FSI Learning Consultation Service, which offers di- agnostic assessment services to all departments and learners. The counseling center uses learning style questionnaires, proficiency information from certified testers and examiners, learner self-reports about strengths/weaknesses and learning experiences, and teacher observations. Diagnostic results and suggestions are conveyed to learners for learning purposes and (with learner permission) to specially trained instructional staff for use with the learners in their continued study.

For learners of Russian, the Specialized Language Training Center in Rockville, Maryland uses a level test based on sophistications in translation, a test for automaticity, assessment using syntactic models, a grammar test, and learning styles feedback. The assessment is expected to determine weaknesses in intra-sentential case usage and functions, aspect, late-acquired verb types (verbs of motion and reflexive verbs), participial phrases & verbal adverbs (also typically late-acquired in Russian), specialized terminology (upon learner request), syntax (which differs significantly from English and commonly taught world languages), sociolinguistic elements (including register), genre, dialectal speech (including standard, substandard and regional forms), cultural allusions, and ellipsis. The diagnostic assessment is also shared with learners to help them understand their strengths, weaknesses, and learning needs, and as a starting point for a learning plan.

A useful diagnostic assessment consists of a number of items. Any one diagnostic procedure will differ from another, but they all have certain things in common. Specifically, most diagnostic assessments include some form of proficiency/performance/competency testing that identifies in a fairly refined manner the strengths and weaknesses in learner language, feedback on learning styles, some form of output (typically, an individualized learning plan), advice to teachers for program/course/lesson adaptation, and some form of sharing of the assessment results with the learner.

Diagnostic teaching, based on the results of diagnostic assessment, can be accomplished at any level of proficiency. At the highest levels, however, from the experience of US government teachers, diagnostic teaching is not an option: it is a mandate.

Further Reading

Cohen, Bella. 2003. *Diagnostic Assessment at the Superior-Distinguished Threshold.* Salinas, CA: MSI Press.

Cohen, Bella. 2004. "Diagnostic Assessment at 3+/4: A Synopsis." *Journal for Distinguished Language Studies 2*: 41-66.

Cohen, Bella. 2004. "Diagnostic Assessment at Superior and Distinguished Levels of Proficiency." In *Teaching and Learning to Near-Native Levels of Language Proficiency: The Proceedings of the Spring and Fall 2003 Conferences of the Coalition of Distinguished Language Centers* (Leaver & Shekhtman, eds.). Salinas, CA: MSI Press.

Ehrman, Madeine. 2001. "Bringing Learning Strategies to the Learner: The FSI Language Learning Consultation Service." In *Language in Our Time: Bilingual Education and Official English, Ebonics and Standard English, Immigration and the Unz Initiative* (Alatis & Tan). Washington, DC: Georgetown University Press.

Ehrman, Madeline, & Leaver, Betty Lou. 2003. "Cognitive Styles in the Service of Language Learning." *System 31* (3): 393-415.

Leaver, Betty Lou. 1992. "From the New Paradigm to the Next Paradigm: Learner-Centered Instruction." *Vision 2020*. Tucson, AZ: AATSEEL.

Leaver, Betty Lou & Aliev, Nizami Nazimov. 1993. "A New Age in Two Lands: The Individual and Individualism in Foreign Language Instruction." In *Learner-Centered Instruction* (Aliev & Leaver). Salinas, CA: The AGSI Press.

Shekhtman, Boris. 2003. *Working with Advanced Language Learners.* Salinas, CA: MSI Press.

38

Develop the Ability to Hear
Natural Error Correction

Betty Lou Leaver
(Defense Language Institute Foreign Language Center)

Natural language correction occurs on many occasions when a non-native speaker converses with a native speaker. Although the native speaker is not a teacher and is not teaching the non-native speaker, correction of a sort does occur, if the non-native speaker listens attentively, because when a native speaker responds to non-native speech, naturally repeating some portion of what has been said when responding, he or she does not repeat the language in- correctly but rather correctly.

As native speakers, when we are corrected, however subtly, in our own language, we recognize the correction. It might be a word, a sociolinguistic blunder, or a cultural faux pas. Typically, we are corrected when our language is not adequately interpretable, i.e. when our interlocutor cannot understand us. Usually when we meet with correction, we note it immediately, often making the correction a permanent part of our linguistic/ sociolinguistic/cultural repertoire. (Sometimes, correction is needed more than once.) Sometimes, we are embarrassed by the mistake we have made, and sometimes, the error is such that we laugh about it with our interlocutor.

Language learners, however, rarely hear these corrections. They are too frequently focused on wording what they have to say, i.e., the mechanics of their speech, to be as mentally open to in- put as needed in order to hear natural error correction. Only at the highest levels do they achieve the ability to multi-task in communication (i.e., speak, listen, remember, and think at the same time). Helping them to learn to listen for natural error correction is a way to speed up their ability to multi-task in a world language.

There are two aspects of natural language correction. One is hearing the corrections, and the other is asking for corrections in natural ways. Both of these aspects usually require direct instruction.

Hearing corrections comes more readily to learners with auditory learning preferences than to others. Those learners who are not natural listeners can be taught to listen for correction indirectly through exercises that are actually intended to teach register; in such exercises, learners make a statement, the teacher puts it into a higher or lower register, and the learner than puts it into a third register. Learning to listen for correction can be taught more directly but spontaneously. When learners miss natural error correction, the teacher can deliberately stop the flow of the conversation (which will focus the learner's attention immediately) and point out that the learner has just been corrected. Any kind of exercise whose goal is the development of attentional focus can be adapted for teaching learners to listen in a more sophisticated way.

Learners are even less likely to know how to ask for clarification. "Please repeat that" is a request that can be accepted from learners at low levels of proficiency but is a conversation stopper at high levels. Obviously, not everything that is said by every native speaker is understood by every other native speaker. Many times speakers are not careful in how they word things, and the information is at best ambiguous and at worse incomprehensible. There are natural ways in which native speakers ask for clarification in such cases. These ways, such as asking for greater detail, repeating the unclear phrase with questioning intonation, and probing ("Just what do you mean by that?"), can be taught through a serious of exercises prepared to give learners the opportunity to practice and repeat these techniques in the classroom and in real-life situations (such as interviews with native speakers that can be set up as extramural events).

Even learners who have achieved native-like proficiency continue to improve their language over time. These two skills—to hear natural corrections and to ask for clarification in unobtrusive ways—will stand them in good stead for lifelong language learning success.

Teachers can teach these skills in their classroom by using natural correction in addition to the typical, overt, teacher correction. In such cases, when the learner does not pick up on the correction, the teacher can point that out.

Further Reading

Leaver, Betty Lou. 2003. *Achieving Native-Like Second-Language Proficiency.* Salinas, CA: MSI Press.

Shekhtman, Boris. 2021. *How to Improve Your Foreign Language Immediately.* Hollister, CA: MSI Press.

Shekhtman, Boris. 2003. *Working with Advanced Foreign Language Learners.* Salinas, CA: MSI Press.

39

Assess High-Level Production the Way We Teach High-Level Production

Thomas Jesús Garza
(University of Texas at Austin)

The adage, "Test the way you teach," may seem to be applicable only at the lower level of instruction and proficiency when learners are still grappling with basic forms of the language and relatively simple communicative tasks. Learners in a proficiency-oriented beginning-level course who have, for example, been regularly exposed to authentic, multi-media and multi-modal forms of presentation and practice of the language and culture in class would be greatly disadvantaged by then having to produce discrete grammatical forms or write out dialogues on a test if those types of production had not been previously practiced in class. Effective assessment of these learners would be better achieved if the testing instrument better reflected what learners had been doing in class all along.

Given the complex and varied format and content of a student-centered proficiency-based high-level course, a single assessment instrument would probably be insufficient for measure accurately the learner's ability to function in the language. Thus, for language learners pursuing professional levels of proficiency, a multi-tiered multi-modal approach to assessing high-level production is both appropriate and effective. Such assessments mimics in form and content the material covered and mastered in class. For instance, if learners have been conducting virtual interviews with peers in country on election trends and voter attitudes in their country, at least part of their overall performance assessment for the course should reflect format of this activity and the language and cultural material mastered as a result. These same learners might also be in the process of preparing a group project the engages speakers of the language from their community. Their project will present a video montage of the members of the community expressing their views on participating in U.S. elections, which will then be narrated and commented on by the members of the group. This project, too, could and should be part of the overall assessment of learners' progress and production in the course.

A multi-tiered assessment model of production at this proficiency level allows the instructor to measure and evaluate learners' performance using the same modalities and formats that have demonstrated in class activities and projects. For most upper-level language courses, this model has three components:

- Proficiency-Based Assessment: Following the models of instruction used in class, proficiency-based assessment, including Oral Proficiency Interviews (OPIs), Writing Proficiency Tests (WPTs), and Simulated Oral Proficiency Interviews (SOPIs) can provide accurate determination of levels of communication and intercultural competence that mimic the process of in-class oral interrogation during and following presentations and/or written writeups of the same projects using instructed-generated prompts. In all cases, the assessment proceeds in a manner that is familiar and known to the learner so that the production phase is minimally interrupted by affective factors.

- Portfolio Assessment: As a component part of out-of-class activities, the language and culture portfolio provide a very learner-centered, self-leveling tool to allow learners to demonstrate competencies particular to their interests, strengths, and identities. The portfolio can be maintained entirely online in a google drive or other file sharing site so that the instructor can periodically access and review the entries compiled a few times during the course. Sample types of entries may be provided to illustrate the typical scope and content of portfolio materials, as well as a scoring rubric that designates the salient ratable features of entries: use of language; amount of language used/produced in the entry; creativity; cultural explications; etc. But it is the learners themselves who are the real engine of this assignment, selecting, developing, and presenting the various entries based on their own interests. The language and culture portfolio can represent a significant part of a more robust assessment of higher-level proficiency.

- Project-Based Assessment: This tool can be directly tied to projects already undertaken in the course, allowing for the assessment to be of production that has been developed during the regular classroom sessions. Smaller-scale projects may be assigned to learners individually, or more ambitious projects can be undertaken by small groups. A rubric for scoring the final project may be presented either "live" in front of the class, or digitally video recorded and uploaded to the class learning management system for final review. Even though the project subjects may be assigned to the learners, each project is developed, scripted, and performed by the individuals, once again allowing for the instrument to be largely student-centered.

Taken as a whole, these three constituent parts of a multi-tiered assessment recreate and reflect the activities, process, and methods of the larger course. They also provide both the instructor and learner a more complete ratable sample of language and culture performance. Notably, what is missing from this assessment toolkit is any kind of achievement or pro-chievement testing of discrete grammatical or lexical items. At this level of proficiency, such assessment is imbedded in the rubrics for the larger instrument, as they are in the higher-level descriptors in the proficiency guidelines themselves. Grammar, lexicon, pronunciation, cultural literacy, etc. are all necessary for successful execution of each project and are, thus, assessed integrally rather than discretely.

By implementing multi-tiered assessment in courses aimed at developing professional proficiency, instructors can obtain more nuanced and accurate assessments of language and culture, while learners enjoy much lowered affective factors surrounding the process of testing and measurement. By testing in the manner we teach, all individuals in the language and culture learning process benefit.

Further Reading

Burner, Tony. 2014. "The Potential Formative Benefits of Portfolio Assessment in Second and Foreign Language Writing Contexts: Review of the Literature." *Studies in Educational Evaluation* 43: 139-149.

Dooly, Melinda. 2012. "Promoting Competency-Based Language Teaching through Project-Based Language Learning." In *Competency-Based Language Teaching in Higher Education*. Maria Luisa Pérez Cañado, ed. Dordrecht: Springer. https://doi.org/10.1007/978-94-007-5386-0

Ross, Stephen. "The Impact of Assessment Method on Foreign Language Proficiency Growth." Applied Linguistics 26(3): 317-342. https://doi.org/10.1093/applin/ami011

Thomas Jesús Garza, Ed. D.

About the Contributors

Rajai Rasheed Al-Khanji (Ph.D., University of Delaware) served as Dean, College of Arts, University of Jordan, Amman from 2002-2006. He was also Chair of Modern Language Department from 1996-1998 at the same university. He has received several research grants from the Fulbright Foundation, the Korea Foundation, and the International Spanish Agency, as well as the Distinguished Research Award in 2005 from the Ministry of Higher Education in Jordan. He served as a senior member on various committees, updating English textbooks for the Jordanian Ministry of Education and worked as a senior interpreter for the American CBC Network office in Jordan during the First Gulf War. From 2003 to the present, he has served as a member of the editorial board of the *Journal for Distinguished Language Studies*.

Olla Al-Shalchi (Ph.D. Old Dominion University) is Assistant Professor of Instruction and Coordinator of the Arabic Program at the University of Texas at Austin. She also has directed the Arabic Summer Institute and develops courses to help prepare learners for their capstone experience in Arabic in Meknes, Morocco. Before joining the University of Texas, she taught at Smith College, Williams College, the American University of Cairo, Middlebury College, the College of William and Mary, and the George Washington University.

James E. Bernhardt (Ph.D., University of Pittsburgh) is an Adjunct Professor of Russian at Northern Virginia Community College and until his recent retirement, Chair of the Department of Near East, Central and South Asian Languages at the Foreign Service Institute (FSI). Prior to that, he was the Russian Language Training Supervisor at FSI and Department Chair of Russian at the College of Wooster and Gustavus Adolphus College.

Gerd Brendel (Ph.D., University of California at Irvine) recently retired from the Defense Language Institute Foreign Language Center where he held a number of different positions, including, but not limited to, Director of the Diagnostic Assessment Center at the Defense Language Institute, testing specialist, and curriculum developer, overseeing the development of intermediate and advanced course instructional materials for a number of languages. Prior to that, he taught at the Bundessprachenamt, the German government's famous language institute.

Tseng Tseng Chang is professor of Chinese at the Defense Language Institute. She has also worked in the curriculum development division as an Online Diagnostic Assessment specialist and curriculum development specialist and in the Provost Office on special research projects. Prior to that, she taught Chinese at Monterey Institute of International Studies. She is co-author of the textbook *Business Chinese* (2005).

Dan Davidson (Ph.D., Harvard University) is President Emeritus and Co-Founder of the American Councils for International Education, including the American Council of Teachers of Russian and Professor Emeritus of Russian and Second Language Acquisition at Bryn Mawr College, where he also served as Department Chair. He currently serves as the Director of the American Councils Research Center and Senior Academic Advisor. He also serves as advisor and consultant to dozens of language programs worldwide, oversees an extensive network of study abroad programs and branch institutional offices in the former Soviet Union, and has maintained the largest database in existence of adult second language acquisition during study abroad in the countries of the former Soviet Union, gathered via a twenty-year longitudinal, empirical. His study, "A Bilingual Associative Dictionary of the

Language of English and Russian Youth," adds to the materials available for those working at high levels of Russian proficiency. Most recently, he co-edited the book, *Transformative Language Learning and Teaching*, published in 2021 by Cambridge University Press.

Antonella Del Fatorre-Olson (M.A., University of Rome) is Distinguished Senior Lecturer in Italian at the University of Texas at Austin, where she coordinates lower-division and supervises Intensive second-year Italian. She collaborated in the writing of several first-year textbooks and workbooks and is co-author of *In viaggio, Moving Toward Fluency in Italian* and its workbook. Every other year, she offers the "Italian Drama Workshop," an upper-division course in Italian in which learners perform plays written by major Italian playwrights; so far, she has directed fifteen plays at UT and fifteen in Rome.

Christian Degueldre (M. A., University of Mons, Belgium) served as Co-Director of the Center for the Advancement of Distinguished Language Proficiency at San Diego State University and Chairman of the Board of the Coalition of Distinguished Language Centers. He is also a professional interpreter, who has worked for several heads of state. He has taught T&I at the Graduate School of Translation and Interpretation at the Monterey Institute of International Studies and as Distinguished Visiting Professor in the Spanish and Portuguese Department and the European Studies Department of San Diego State University, where he continues to serve as a consultant while working professionally in Europe.

Madeline Ehrman, d.2015, (Ph.D., Union Institute) was an international language learning consultant. She spent a career at the Foreign Service Institute, US Department of State, where she established and directed the Research, Evaluation, and Development division, founding there the Learning Consultation Service. At FSI, she also served as Department Chair of Asian and African Languages and completed much original research on the development of nativelike language skills. She was also a Senior Fellow at the National Foreign Language Center and a Senior Researcher at the Center for the Advanced Study of Language.

Karen Evans-Romaine (Ph.D. University of Michigan) is Professor of Russian at the University of Wisconsin – Madison and Co-Director of the Russian Language Flagship. She directed the Kathryn Wasserman Davis School of Russian at Middlebury College from 2003–2009 and coordinated the first-year Russian program there from 2001–2003. She is co-author with Richard Robin and Galina Shatallina of the two-volume elementary Russian language textbook *Golosa*, and co-editor with Dianna Murphy of a collection of articles on Flagship programs, *Exploring the US Language Flagship Program: Professional Competence in a Second Language by Graduation* (2016).

Vivian Flanzer (Ph.D., University of Texas at Austin) is a Senior Lecturer in the Department of Spanish and Portuguese at the University of Texas at Austin, where she serves as the coordinator of the Portuguese language program and, since 2018, as Associate Director of the UT Portuguese Flagship Program. She is the author of the interactive website and accompanying textbook, *ClicaBrasil: Portuguese Language and Culture for Intermediate Students* (2019).

Surendra Gambhir (Ph.D., University of Pennsylvania) has previously taught at the University of Pennsylvania, Cornell University and University of Wisconsin at Madison. He was the Chair of Language Committee of the American Institute of Indian Studies from 1998-2007 and has directed overseas programs in twelve Indic languages. He has directed many national projects and is the author of six books and numerous articles in the areas of sociolinguistics and language pedagogy. He is currently an adjunct Associate Professor at the University of Pennsylvania and is the director of Institute of Language Study and Research based in Philadelphia, PA.

Thomas Jesús Garza (Ed.D., Harvard University) is UT Regents' and University Distinguished Teaching Associate Professor of Slavic and Eurasian Studies at the University of Texas at Austin and Director of the Texas Language Center. He coordinated the Russian program at U Texas from 1990 to 2010 and directed the Arabic Flagship program between 2015-2018. He has co-authored several textbooks of English as a Foreign Language and Russian, as well as the *World-Readiness Standards for Russian* (2020) with Jane Shuffelton and Peter Merrill.

Peter Glanville (Ph.D., University of Texas at Austin) is Associate Professor and Director of the Arabic Language Flagship program at the University of Maryland – College Park. His research focus is Arabic linguistics and Arabic language pedagogy. His book, *The Lexical Semantics of the Arabic Verb*, was published in 2018.

Jiaying Howard (Ph.D., UC Santa Barbara) is Editor of *Applied Language Learning* and *Dialogue on Language Instruction*. Previously, she served as Dean of the Immersion Language Office at the Defense Language Institute. Prior to that, she was a long-time professor of Chinese at Monterey Institute of International Studies, where she also served as the MIIS representative to the Coalition of Distinguished Language Centers.

Frederick Jackson (Ph.D., University of Hawaii) is a Senior Research Associate at the National Foreign Language Center. Prior to that, he headed the International Language Roundtable for more than seven years and held several posts (Language Training Supervisor of 18 language programs, including Thai, Albanian, Burmese, Hebrew and Germans, and founder and head of the Staff Development Program, among others) at the Foreign Service Institute, from which he has now retired.

Orlando Kelm (Ph.D., University of California - Berkeley) is Associate Professor of Hispanic Linguistics and, since 2018, the Director of the Portuguese Flagship at the University of Texas at Austin. His professional interests center on the use language and culture for professional purposes, such as Business Spanish and Portuguese. His current research focuses on the creation of instructional materials, including the use of innovative technologies in foreign language instruction. His most recent book, *The Seven Keys to Communicating in Mexico: An Intercultural Approach*, was published in 2020.

Cornelius Kubler (Ph.D., Cornell University; M.A. National Taiwan University) is Stanfield Professor of Asian Studies and Chair of the Department of Asian Studies at Williams College. Earlier, he served as Scientific Linguist in Mandarin, Cantonese, Japanese, and Mongolian and as Chair of the Department of Asian and African Languages at the Foreign Service Institute. From 1981 to 1987, he was Principal of the American Institute in Taiwan Chinese Language and Area Studies School, where he directed long-term, intensive language training programs designed to bring adult American and European learners from Advanced to Superior, and from Superior to Distinguished proficiency.

Betty Lou Leaver (Ph.D., Pushkin Institute, Moscow) is retired as Provost at the Defense Language Institute Foreign Language Center where she previously served as an associate provost and dean. Since retiring, and concurrently with other positions for several decades, she has served as an international educational consultant and has assisted ministries of education in 24 countries. She has also served as academic dean and chief academic officer at New York Institute of Technology in Jordan, where she also taught discourse analysis at the University of Jordan, founded the Jordan Consortium for Distinguished Language Studies, and served as Executive Director of the Coalition of Distinguished Language Centers. She has overseen advanced language programs at the Foreign Service Institute,

NASA, and the American Global Studies Institute. Together with Claudia Angelelli, Mary Ann Lyman Hager, and Christian Degueldre, she co-founded the Center for the Advancement of Distinguished Language Proficiency at San Diego State University, and together with William Fierman and Roxana Ma Newman, she co-founded the Center for the Languages of the Central Asian Region (CeLCAR) at Indiana University.

Maria Lekič (Ph.D., University of Pennsylvania) retired from the University of Maryland at College Park. She is director of the American Council of Teachers of Russian's academic division of testing and curriculum development, and also oversees the National Flagship Program for learners reaching past advanced levels of Russian. She is author or co-author of several of the major textbook materials used today in the United States at the college and pre-college level, including *Russian Stage One: Live from Russia!* vols. 1 and 2.

Natalia Lord (M.A., Fordham University) retired as a specialist in learner counseling at the Research, Evaluation, and Development Center at the Foreign Service Institute, US Department of State. Together with Boris Shekhtman, she developed the first advanced ("Beyond Three") Russian course at FSI in 1984. She also taught Russian at Howard University.

Cindy Martin (Ph.D., University of Pennsylvania) is Associate Professor and Department Head at the University of Maryland - College Park, where she also serves as Undergraduate Program Director for Russian and Director of the Russian Domestic Flagship Program. She is author of *Welcome Back! Russian Stage Two* (2001) and contributing editor of *Beyond the Oral Proficiency Workshop: Resources for Teaching, Learning, and Testing for Proficiency* (2007).

Michael Morrissey (Ph.D., Cornell University), now retired, was a lecturer in English as a Foreign Language at the University of Kassel, Germany and served as the university's representative to the Coalition of Distinguished Language Centers.

Richard Robin (Ph.D., University of Michigan) is Professor of Russian and International Affairs and Director of the Russian Language program at the George Washington University. He is the author or co-author of numerous Russian language textbooks, including *Golosa: A Beginning Course in Russian* (1993-2013), *Political Russian* (1991-2009), and *Russian for Russians* (1991-2006), among others. He also coordinates distance learning projects using authentic language materials on the Internet.

Maria Shardakova (Ph.D., Bryn Mawr College) is Associate Professor and Russian Language Program Director at Indiana University, where she also serves as Director of the IU Russian Flagship program. Her teaching is closely tied with and informed by her research in second language methodology, pedagogy, and assessment. She is currently working on two collaborative initiatives: creating instructional materials in Open Educational Resources and developing online materials for Russian language tutors.

Boris Shekhtman, d. 2017. (M.A. Grozny Pedagogical Institute) was president of the Specialized Language Training Center and Operations Manager of the Coalition of Distinguished Language Centers. He taught Russian through near-native levels and trained teachers in the United States and other countries to do the same. Prior to founding his own language institute, he taught Russian for many years at the Foreign Service Institute, where, with Natalia Lord, he developed the first advanced Russian ("Beyond Three") course in 1984.

Kenneth Shepard has directed language test development at the National Foreign Language Center at the University of Maryland, having previously served as the associate director of TOEFL for research. Today, he heads a team managing the English language program at the seven Colleges of Technology in the Sultanate of Oman.

Svetlana Sibrina (M.A., Chelyabinsk State Pedagogical University) is an Associate Professor at of Russian at the Defense Language Institute Foreign Language Center. She has also taught at Howard University, the School of Advanced International Studies at Johns Hopkins University, and the George Washington University. She has published a number of articles on language learning at the near-native level and co-authored the *Sociolinguistic Workbook for Students Studying toward the Distinguished Level of Proficiency* under the auspices of the Coalition of Distinguished Language Centers and funded by the U.S. Department of Education.

Irina Walsh (Ph.D., Bryn Mawr College) is Lecturer and Co-Director of the Russian Language Flagship at Bryn Mawr College. She is also Co-Director of the summer Russian Language Institute at Bryn Mawr, at which she is also an instructor. Prior to her appointment at Bryn Mawr, she taught Russian language, film, and culture at Temple University and at the College of New Jersey.

Other MSI Publications
in Foreign Language & Culture

Achieving Native-Like Second-Language Proficiency: A Catologue of Critical Factors: Volume 1: Speaking (Leaver)

Communicative Focus: Teaching Foreign Language on the Basis of the Native Speaker's Communicative Focus (Shekhtman & Kupchankas)

Damascus amid the War (M. Imady)

Diagnostic Assessment at the Superior/Distinguished Threshold (Cohen)

Día de Muertos (Sula)

Good Blood (Schaffer)

How to Improve Your Foreign Language Immediately (Shekhtman)

Individualized Study Plans for Very Advanced Students of Foreign Languages (Leaver)

Journal for Distinguished Language Studies

Living in Blue Sky Mind (Diedrichs)

Methods of Individualization in Teaching Foreign Languages, Based on the Influence of Cognitive Styles on Language Acquisition (Leaver)

Road to Damascus (I. Imady)

Syrian Folktales (M. Imady)

Teaching and Learning to Near-Native Levels of Language Proficiency (Leaver & Shekhtman)

Teaching and Learning to Near-Native Levels of Language Proficiency II (Robin & Dubinsky)

Teaching and Learning to Near-Native Levels of Language Proficiency III (Dubinsky & Butler)

Teaching and Learning to Near-Native Levels of Language Proficiency IV (Butler & Zhou)

The Invisible Foreign Language Classroom (Dabbs & Leaver)

The Rise and Fall of Muslim Civil Society (O. Imady)

The Subversive Utopia: Louis Kahn and the Question of the National Jewish Style in Jerusalem (Sakr)

Think Yourself into Becoming a Language Learning Super Star (Leaver)

Thoughts without a Title (Henderson)

Travels with Elly: Reflections on Canada by an RVer and His Dog (MacDonald)

What Works: Helping Students Reach Native-Like Second-Language Competence (CDLC; the earlier version of *Practices That Work*)

When You're Shoved from the Right, Look to Your Left: Metaphors of Islamic Humanism (O. Imady)

Working with Advanced Foreign Language Students (Shekhtman)